English Simplified

Fourth Canadian Edition

Blanche Ellsworth

John A. Higgins

Arnold Keller
University of Victoria

Longman

Toronto

National Library of Canada Cataloguing in Publication Data

Ellsworth, Blanche, 1902–
    English simplified

4th Canadian ed.
ISBN 0-321-10154-5

     1. English Language—Grammar. 2. English Language—Punctuation. I. Keller, Arnold
II. Higgins, John A. III. Title.

PE1112.E43 2003   428.2   C2001-902795-8

ISBN 0-321-10154-5

Vice President, Editorial Director: Michael Young
Acquisitions Editor: David Stover
Marketing Manager: Sharon Loeb
Developmental Editor: Meaghan Eley
Production Editor: Cheryl Jackson
Copy Editor: Ann McInnis
Production Coordinator: Peggy Brown
Page Layout: Christine Velakis
Art Director: Julia Hall
Cover Design: Amy Harnden
Cover Image: Comstock

  2 3 4 5   06 05 04 03 02

Printed and bound in Canada.

Contents

Preface

The fourth Canadian edition of *English Simplified* continues to provide students with clear and comprehensive advice about writing. As before, we have focussed on those specific skills that our readers tell us concern them most, ensuring that *English Simplified* remains a valuable adjunct to the classroom. Many years of gratifying responses from both instructors and students confirm that we're on the right track.

We have revised examples throughout and clarified explanations as needed, all the while maintaining a distinctively Canadian voice. Again, we draw on Canada's heritage, politics, arts, and sports to provide student writers with a familiar context in which to learn.

We've also revised the accompanying workbook, *Exercises for English Simplified*, reflecting Canadian life at the start of a new millennium. As in the past, readers will find thousands of practice questions conveniently keyed to specific sections of the main text. An answer key is available for instructors.

Once more, it is a pleasure to thank the students, instructors, and others whose invaluable support has helped shape the Canadian edition of *English Simplified*, including reviewers A.J. Mittendorf, College of New Caledonia, and Zoe Hurley, Grant MacEwan College.

Arnold Keller
The University of Victoria

The Crown charged Raines with leaving the scene of an accident in a three-count indictment.

A computer can exasperate novice users when they beep and flash error messages.

Five earthquake victims were buried ten times as many remained in hospitals.

Can you tell what is wrong with each of these sentences? Well-intentioned adults too often write sentences like these, thinking them clear and correct. Without an understanding of the basic grammar of the English sentence, we can easily fall into such pitfalls of language. This part of *English Simplified* explains basic grammar concisely, in the most common terms, to help you create sentences that are clear, correct, and effective.

1–3. The Sentence and Its Parts

The sentence is our basic unit of spoken or written thought. In writing, a sentence begins with a capital letter and ends with a period, question mark, or exclamation point. Every sentence consists of two essential parts, called **subject** and **predicate**.

1. The Two Parts of a Sentence

A. The Subject. The subject part of a sentence (called the **complete subject**) is the part that names the person or thing the sentence speaks about. That person or thing itself is called the **simple subject** (usually shortened to just **subject**). In the examples below, the complete subject is boxed and the simple subject is in **bold print**.

> A vicious **blizzard** swept through the valley.
>
> Three **friends** from high school rented a room in Regina.
>
> Canadian foreign **policy** toward China was a lively topic.
>
> **Glenn Gould** has left an indelible mark on Canadian music.

Note: Only the most common kind of sentence, the kind that *tells*, is shown here. In Section 3A you will meet sentences that *ask*, *command*, and *exclaim*. For simplicity, most sentence discussions in this book will deal with sentences that tell (declarative sentences).

B. The Predicate. The predicate part of a sentence (called the **complete predicate**) tells what the subject *does (did, will do)* or what or how the subject *is (was, will be)*. The key word(s) in the predicate—the word(s) stating the actual doing or being—is called the **simple predicate**, or **verb**. In the examples below, the complete predicate is boxed and the simple predicate, or verb, is in **bold**.

> A vicious blizzard **swept** through the valley.
>
> Three friends from high school **rented** a room in Regina.
>
> Canadian foreign policy toward China **was** a lively topic.
>
> Glenn Gould **has left** an indelible mark on Canadian music.

Some complete predicates contain **complements** (words needed to complete the verb's meaning):

> Three friends rented a *room* . . .
>
> Canadian foreign policy . . . was a lively *topic.*
>
> Glenn Gould has left an indelible *mark* . . .

Subjects and complements are explained fully in 11, page 4; verbs are explained in 12–15, pages 5–11.

Note: A subject, verb, or complement may be **compound**; that is, it may have two or more parts joined by *and, or,* or *but*:

> **Subject**   **Predicate**   **Complement**
>
> *Poems* and *stories delight* and *edify children, teenagers,* and *adults.*

2. The Sentence Pattern.
Subject, verb, and **complement(s)** usually occur in a standard order or pattern: **S V (C) (C).** This means that the subject [S] comes first, then the verb [V], then—perhaps—one or two complements [C].

>   s   v
> The risky mission succeeded perfectly.
>
>   s   v   c
> Such rocks emit radiation.
>
>   s   v   c   c
> That noise from the street gave her a headache.

This normal order is altered in most questions (*What did they see?* [→ *They did see what*]) and exclamations (*Such a fool I was!* [→ *I was such a fool*]), and in sentences such as *Never had the company faced such losses* [→ *The company had never faced such losses*] and *There were no seats left* [→ *No seats were left*].

3. Ways of Classifying Sentences

A. By Purpose

> ***Declarative*** (a statement): The day dawned clear.
>
> ***Interrogative*** (a question): Did the day dawn clear?
>
> ***Imperative*** (a command or request): Wake up and greet the day. [*You* is understood to be the subject.]
>
> ***Exclamatory*** (an expression of emotion, usually beginning with *how* or *what*): What a clear day this is! How far we can see!

B. By Structure, according to the number and kinds of clauses they contain. A sentence may be **simple, compound, complex,** or **compound-complex**. Section 22C, page 17, explains these categories in detail.

4–9. The Parts of Speech: A Survey

Every word performs one of five functions: *naming, expressing doing or being, modifying, connecting,* or *expressing emotion*. In traditional grammar, these functions are classified into eight **parts of speech**: *noun, pronoun, verb, adjective, adverb, preposition, conjunction,* and *interjection*.

4. Words That Name

A. Nouns. A noun is a word that names a person, place, or thing (including a quality or idea):

> **Person:** woman, Sandra, poet, Lorna Crozier
>
> **Place:** kitchen, city, park, Mount Royal
>
> **Thing:** tree, ship, HMCS *Calgary*, cereal
>
> **Quality or idea:** love, height, democracy, motion

See 10–11, pages 4–5, for details about nouns.

B. Pronouns (*pro-* means "for" or "instead of"). As its name suggests, a pronoun takes the place of (stands for) a noun. The noun that a pronoun stands for is called the antecedent of that pronoun:

> [antecedent in *italics;* pronoun in **bold**]
>
> *Rosa* brought a friend with **her** to the rally.
>
> If *teams* can't practise at the Memorial Arena, **they** practise in the Archie Browning Centre.

See 18–20, pages 13–15, for details about pronouns.

5. Words That Express Doing or Being: Verbs.

A verb asserts something about the subject of a sentence. An **action verb** tells what the subject *does, did,* or *will do*. A **linking verb** tells that the subject *is, was,* or *will be* something.

> **Action:** Hummingbirds *fly* up to 95 km per hour. [tells what the subject, *Hummingbirds,* does]
>
> **Linking:** The hummingbird *is* nature's helicopter. [tells that the subject is something]

Some verbs consist of several words: a **main verb** preceded by one or more **auxiliary** (helping) **verbs:**

> [auxiliary verbs in *italics;* main verb in **bold**]
>
> Hummingbirds *will* **explore** almost anything red.
>
> They *have* even *been* **attracted** to red ribbons.

The verb in a sentence is also called the **simple predicate**. See 12–15, pages 5–11, for details about verbs.

> *Note:* Besides asserting (in a declarative or exclamatory sentence), a verb can also *ask* (in an interrogative sentence), or *command or request* (in an imperative sentence).

6. Words That Modify.

To *modify* means "to change." A word that modifies changes or clarifies our concept of another word.

A. Adjectives. An adjective modifies a noun (or occasionally a pronoun). It describes that noun or limits its meaning. **Descriptive adjectives** tell *what kind: small* car (what kind of car?), *green* rug, *unimaginable* brutality, *odoriferous 20-cent* cigar. **Limiting adjectives** (determiners) tell *which one* or *how many*. There are several kinds of limiting adjectives.

> **Possessive:** *my* car, *her* grades, *their* policy [which car, grades, policy?]
>
> **Demonstrative:** *this* car, *those* grades, *that* policy
>
> **Indefinite:** *any* car, *either* grade, *many* policies
>
> **Interrogative:** *which* car? *whose* grades? *what* policy?
>
> **Numerical:** *one* car, *two* grades, *third* policy
>
> **Articles:** *a* car, *the* grades, *a* policy

As these examples show, an adjective usually appears directly before the noun it modifies. A descriptive adjective can appear also after a linking verb (as a complement). Such an adjective describes the subject to which the verb links it:

>   S V   C
>
> That song is *lively*. [*Lively* describes the subject, *song*.]
>
> The statistics seemed *reliable*.

B. Adverbs. An adverb usually modifies a verb. It describes *how, when, where,* or *to what degree* the action of a verb is done. There are several kinds of adverbs:

> **Manner:** Meghan dances *gracefully*. [dances how?]
>
> **Time:** Meghan danced *yesterday*. [danced when?]
>
> **Place:** Meghan dances *everywhere*. [dances where?]
>
> **Degree:** Meghan dances *excessively*. [dances to what extent or degree?]

An adverb phrase or clause can also describe *why:* Meghan dances *to keep in condition*. (Sections 21–22, pages 15–17, explain phrases and clauses.)

Some adverbs can modify an adjective or another adverb. Such adverbs are called adverbs of degree (or intensifiers or qualifiers):

> Meghan dances *quite* gracefully. [gracefully to what degree? how gracefully?] Meghan prefers *very* fast music.

For **conjunctive adverbs**, see 39B, page 29.

ESL

Prepositions of Time, Place, and Travel

	At	On	In
Time	a specific time: *at* 9:45, *at* noon	a day or date: *on* Monday, *on* May 5th	a longer time: *in* a week, *in* two months, *in* 2005
Place	a particular spot: *at* home, *at* work, *at* the store, *at* 5th and Main, *at* the end	the top or surface of: *on* Main Street, *on* Vancouver Island	within an area: *in* jail, *in* her office, *in* Alberta, *in* China, *in* bed
Means of Travel		*on* a bike, *on* a bus, *on* a ship, *on* a plane	*in* a car, *in* a carriage, *in* a canoe

7. Words That Connect

A. Conjunctions. A conjunction joins other words or word groups. There are two kinds of conjunctions:

(1) A coordinating conjunction (*and, but, or, nor, for, yet, so*) joins words or word groups of the same kind and same importance:

> ***Words:*** Margaret *and* Pierre
>
> ***Word groups (phrases):*** after their marriage *but* before his final illness
>
> ***Word groups (clauses):*** Pierre lived in Montreal, *but* Margaret preferred Ottawa.

Note: And, but, or, or *nor* may be used with other words to form a **correlative conjunction**: *not only . . . but also; (n)either . . . (n)or; both . . . and:*

> *Both* Margaret and Pierre disliked crowds.
> *Neither* Margaret *nor* Pierre sought the limelight.

See 81, pages 45–47, on using *so.*

(2) A subordinating conjunction (*if, because, although, when, unless,* etc.) joins a dependent (subordinate) clause to an independent (main) clause. The subordinating conjunction begins the dependent clause: *if the heat continues; because repair crews arrived late and with insufficient equipment:*

> The road may buckle *if the heat continues.*
>
> *If the heat continues,* the road may buckle.
>
> Traffic was delayed across much of the West End *because repair crews arrived late and with insufficient equipment.*
>
> *Because repair crews arrived late and with insufficient equipment,* traffic was delayed across much of the West End.

Do not write a subordinate clause alone as if it were a sentence:

> ***Wrong:*** The road may buckle. If the heat continues.

Section 26A, pages 21–22, discusses this serious error (a *fragment*).

Other common subordinating conjunctions are *after, as, as if, as soon as, as though, before, in order that, provided, since, so that, than, though, until, whenever, where, whereas, wherever, whether, while.* See 22B(2), page 17.

Note: Other kinds of words that join clauses are **relative pronouns** (such as *who* or *which*—see 22B(1), page 16) and **conjunctive adverbs** (such as *therefore* or *however*—see 39B, page 29).

B. Prepositions. A preposition is a connecting word such as *in, on, of, for,* or *into* that shows how a noun is related to the sentence containing it:

> The plane flew *over* the clouds.
>
> The plane flew *into* the clouds.
>
> The plane flew *through* the clouds.

Each preposition above shows a different relation between the noun *clouds* and the action of the sentence. Other common prepositions are:

about	by	out (of)
above	despite	outside
against	down	past
among	during	since
as	except	through (out)
as well as	from	to
at	inside	toward
because of	instead of	under
before	in addition to	underneath
behind	in front of	until
below	like	up
beneath	near	upon
beside	next to	within
besides	off	without
between	onto	

The word group beginning with the preposition and ending with the noun is called a **prepositional phrase**. The noun (or pronoun) is called the **object of the preposition**:

> [preposition in **bold**; object of preposition in *italics*]
>
> **behind** her cheery *façade* **of** his *memories* **with** *us*

8. Words That Express Emotion: Interjections.

Unlike the other kinds of words, the interjection has little or no grammatical connection with the rest of the sentence:

> ***Mild interjection*** (punctuated with comma): *Oh,* I don't care. *Well,* Dr. Vachon might know.
>
> ***Strong interjection*** (punctuated with exclamation point): *Rats!* He's cheated us. *Wow!* It's snowing.

9. Words as More than One Part of Speech.

The way a word is used in a particular sentence determines its part of speech in that sentence. To determine the part of speech of a word in a particular sentence, examine its grammatical use (**syntax**) in that sentence: If it names something, it is a noun; if it describes a noun, it is an adjective; and so forth:

> ***Noun:*** We could see the first *light* of dawn.
>
> ***Verb:*** They would *light* signal fires that night.
>
> ***Adjective:*** Wearing *light* colours enhances visibility.

Note: You can often determine a word's part of speech by its position or its ending. For example, a word following a limiting adjective (*a, my, this,* etc.) is likely to be a noun: *my* **brother**, *this* **test** (another adjective may intervene: *this* impossible **test**). A word following an auxiliary verb is likely to be a verb: *has* **grown**, *might have been* **saved** (an adverb may intervene: *has* hardly **grown**). Most words with an *-ly* ending are adverbs: *slowly, awkwardly;* words ending in *-tion, -ity, -ness, -ment, -hood,* or *-cy* are usually nouns; words ending in *-ify* or *-ize* are probably verbs; words ending in *-al, -ous, -ful,* or *-less* are probably adjectives.

10–11. Using Nouns

Recall that nouns name persons, places, or things.

10. The Kinds of Nouns. Nouns are classified in several ways:

A. Singular or Plural. A **singular** noun names one person, place, or thing: *woman, city, house, chair.* A **plural** noun names two or more persons, places, or things: *women, cities, houses, chairs.* Most singular nouns become plural by the addition of *s.* See 72, pages 42–43, for rules on the formation of plurals.

B. Common or Proper. A **common** noun names one or more members of a class of things: *woman, women, mice, city, chair, auditorium.* A **proper** noun names a specific person, place, or thing: *Tom Connors, Mickey Mouse, Singapore, Notre Dame Cathedral.*

C. Concrete or Abstract. A **concrete** noun names an object that can be perceived by the senses: *woman, Adrienne Clarkson, mice, cheese.* An **abstract** noun names a quality or idea: *liberty, sadness, ambition, love, tragedy, height.*

D. Collective. A **collective** noun names a group of things: *jury, team, flock, committee, army.*

E. Count or Non-count. See 16E (2), page 11–12.

11. The Main Uses of Nouns. Recall the basic sentence pattern: S V (C) (C). That is, each sentence has a subject, a verb, and possibly one or two complements. The subject and the complements are usually nouns.

A. Subject of a Sentence. Pattern: **S** V (C) (C). The **subject** tells *who* or *what* if placed before the verb:

> The *judge* imposed a heavy fine. [Who imposed?]
>
> Both *projects* were abandoned. [What were abandoned?]
>
> *Duff* and *Fong* began the project. [Who began? (compound subject)]

B. Complement. A complement is a word in the complete predicate that completes the meaning of the verb. There are four kinds of complements:

(1) A direct object is a noun (or pronoun) that tells *whom* or *what* after an action verb. Usual pattern: S V C:

> Duff assembled the *equipment.* [assembled what?]
>
> Fong is training *workers.* [training whom?]

(2) An indirect object is a noun (or pronoun) that appears after certain action verbs, telling *to* or *for whom,* or *to* or *for what,* the action of the verb is done. Pattern: S V C (ind. obj.) C (dir. obj.):

> The mayor sent her *aide* a gift. [sent to whom?]
>
> The aide had done the *mayor* a favour. [done for whom?]

(3) A subjective complement (also called a *predicate nominative*) is a noun (or pronoun) that follows a linking verb and renames or explains the subject. Pattern: S V (link) C:

> Felicia Gray is the head *programmer.* [*Programmer* gives another name or title for *Felicia Gray.*]
>
> A tuque is a *hat.* [*Hat* explains what *tuque* is.]

Note: An adjective can also be a subjective complement: Ms. Gray is highly *competent.*

For a full list of linking verbs, see 13C, pages 5–6.

(4) An objective complement is a noun that follows a direct object and renames or explains it. Pattern: S V C (dir. obj.) C (obj. comp.):

Everyone considers Ms. Gray an *expert*. [*Expert* gives another name or title for *Ms. Gray*.]

The director called her appointment a *godsend*.

The objective complement occurs most commonly with such verbs as *call, name, designate, elect, consider, appoint, think*.

> *Note:* An adjective can also be an objective complement: The director called her appointment *fortunate*.

C. An Object of a Preposition is a noun (or pronoun) that ends a prepositional phrase and answers the question *whom* or *what* after the preposition:

> Ms. Roy met with her *publisher* . [with whom?]
> Stores in *town* struggle against new *malls* . [in what? against what?]

D. An Appositive is a noun that closely follows another noun and renames or further identifies that other noun:

> Ms. Gray, the head *programmer,* knows the language. [*Programmer* is another name or title for *Ms. Gray*. It is an appositive (or *in apposition*) to *Ms. Gray*.]
> They hoped the new year, *2001,* would bring peace.

E. Direct Address. A noun (or pronoun) in **direct address** names the person being spoken to:

> *Noun: Derek,* the manager wants to see you.
> *Pronoun:* Get over here, *you!*

12–15. Using Verbs

A verb is the core of every sentence. Without a verb, a group of words is only a fragment of a sentence instead of a complete sentence. Even if a sentence contains only one word, that word must be a verb: *Run! Wait.* (Every verb must have a subject, expressed or understood. In sentences such as *Run!* and *Wait,* the subject is understood to be *you.*) The function of a verb is to assert something about its subject—that is, to tell what the subject *does (did, will do)* or that the subject *is (was, will be)* something (in interrogative sentences the verb will *ask,* and in imperative sentences it will *command* or *request*):

> The storm *raged.*
> Emergency vehicles *were racing* through the streets.
> Power *was* out for hours in several areas of the city.
> Where *were* the emergency vehicles *going?*
> [You] *Prepare* for a long, cold night.

12. Identifying the Verb. There is a simple way to identify the verb in a sentence. The verb is the word that will usually change its form if you change the time of the sentence:

This week they *plan* the budget. Last week they *planned* the budget. Next week they *will plan* the budget. For the last five years they *have planned* the budget.

13. The Kinds of Verbs. A verb is classified according to the kind of complement (if any) that follows it. In addition, there is a special kind of verb called an **auxiliary** (or helping) verb that may accompany a main verb.

A. A Transitive Verb is one that needs a direct object to complete its meaning. That is, it expresses an action that passes across (transits) from a "doer" (the subject—the person or thing that does the action) to a "receiver" (the direct object—the person or thing upon whom the action is done).

> Dr. Spector *removed* the tumour. [*Dr. Spector* did the action, removing; *tumour* (direct object) received the action.]
> Red lights *stop* traffic. [*Lights* do the action; *traffic* receives the action.]

B. An Intransitive Verb is one that does not need a direct object to complete its meaning. It expresses an action that does not have a receiver:

> The meeting *adjourned.*
> The chairperson *stayed* after the meeting. [*After the meeting* is a prepositional phrase, telling when. It is not a direct object.]
> Pollutants *act* insidiously. [*Insidiously* is an adverb, telling how. It is not a direct object.]

> *Note:* Many verbs can be transitive in some uses and intransitive in others. Dictionaries label each meaning of a verb as *v.t. (verb, transitive)* or *v.i. (verb, intransitive).*

C. A Linking (State-of-Being, Copulative) Verb expresses no action at all. It merely expresses state of being; it indicates a link of identity or description between the subject and the subjective complement following the verb:

> Borneo *is* an island. [*Borneo = island.*]
> The Acadians *have been* industrious. [*Industrious* describes Acadians.]
> Her cousin *became* a minister. [*Cousin = minister.*]

The chief linking verb is *be.* Its parts are:

am	is	are	was	were	being	been

Other linking verbs are those roughly like *be* in meaning—

seem	appear	remain	prove	become	grow	turn

—and the verbs of the five senses:

look	sound	feel	smell	taste

Some verbs may be linking verbs in one sense and action verbs in another:

Linking	Action
I *looked* dishevelled.	I *looked* out the window.
Mitsuko *grew* pensive.	Mitsuko *grew* cabbages.

D. Auxiliary (Helping) Verbs. A verb may contain more than one word, as in *could have helped.* The last word in the verb is the **main verb.** The others are called auxiliary verbs, or simply **auxiliaries.** They convey some condition of the main verb, such as tense or mood.

Only a few verbs can be auxiliaries:

have	shall	might
be (am, is, . . .)	should	must
do	can	have to
will	could	ought (to)
would	may	need (to)

All except *have, be,* and *do* are called **modal auxiliaries,** or just **modals.** Generally, modals work like *will* and *would* (see 14B (3), (6), (7), pages 7–8.): He *will* go. He *might* go. He *ought to* go. He *might* have gone. He *could have been* going.

After *be,* the main verb uses its present participle (*-ing* form): *is flying.* After *have,* the main verb uses its past participle (*-ed* or irregular form): *has departed, had gone* (for more on participles, see 14A below; 14D (2), page 9, and 15D, page 10):

> The plane **is flying** here non-stop.
>
> The plane **will be** landing soon.
>
> The plane **had** departed from Saint John.
>
> The plane **did** arrive on time.
>
> The plane **should** arrive on time.
>
> The plane **must** certainly **have** landed by now.[Note that other words may come between parts of the verb.]
>
> **Would** any of the planes **have** landed sooner?

Note: Verbs of more than one word are sometimes called **verb phrases.**

14. Using Verbs Correctly

A. Know the Three Principal Parts of Verbs. The **principal parts** are the parts you need to know to form all of a verb's tenses (time forms):

| ESL | | | |

Principal Part	Present Tense	Past Tense	Past Participle
Regular verb	walk	walked	walked
Irregular verb	see	saw	seen

Regular verbs form their past tense and past participle by adding *-ed* to the present (with some minor spelling changes, as in *stopped, cried*). Irregular verbs form these parts in

various ways, such as *broken, thought, sung, made, swum.* See 15D, page 10, for forms of many irregular verbs. Consult your dictionary when in doubt about others, for you cannot safely take one irregular verb as a model for another; consider *make (made, made)* and *take (took, taken).*

> *Note:* Some texts and dictionaries list a fourth principal part, the **present participle,** formed with *-ing* added to the present form: *seeing, playing.* It is always regular, except for some minor spelling changes (*stopping, loving*).

B. Use the Correct Verb Tense and Form. *Tense* refers to time; verbs use different tense forms when expressing different times. Among all its tenses, English has only three common verb endings: *-s* (sometimes *-es*), *-ed* (sometimes *-d*), and *-ing.* Proofread your writing very carefully to be sure you never omit these endings.

> *Note:* Verb forms are often listed by **person.** In grammar, there are three persons: the *first person* means the person(s) doing the speaking: *I* or *we.* The *second person* means the person being spoken to: *you.* The *third person* means the person or thing being spoken about: *he, she, it, they,* or any noun, such as *house, athletes, Horace.* For the meaning of *singular* and *plural,* see 10A, page 4.

(1) The present tense

- **The basic present tense form** (using the first principal part). Note where the *-s* ending occurs:

	Singular	Plural
First person	I walk	we walk
Second person	you walk	you walk
Third person	he/she/it walk**s**	they walk

Use this form for an action that happens regularly or always: I usually *watch* the late news. Beth *drives* a minivan. The sun *sets* in the west. Use this form also usually with *be, have,* and verbs of mental action, emotion, and the senses—such as *see, hear, think, understand, mean, feel, know*—for something happening at the present moment (I *am* ready. They *have* coffee. I *hear* a plane. She *understands* it. They *know* the way.)

- **The present progressive form.** Note the *-ing* ending:

	Singular	Plural
First person	I am walk**ing**	we are walk**ing**
Second person	you are walk**ing**	you are walk**ing**
Third person	he/she/it is walk**ing**	they are walk**ing**

With most verbs, use this form to stress that something is in progress at the present moment: Right now

I *am* (or I'*m*) *exercising*. She *is* (or She'*s*) *travelling* today. Use the progressive also in questions (and their answers) and negatives as follows: *Are* you *walking*? *Is* she *walking*? *Are* the Smiths *coming*? I *am* (or I'*m*) not *walking*. She *is* (or She'*s*) not *walking*. The Smiths *are* not (or *aren*'t) *coming*.

- **The present emphatic form:**

	Singular	Plural
First person	I do walk	we do walk
Second person	you do walk	you do walk
Third person	he/she/it does walk	they do walk

Use this form in almost all other questions (and their answers) and negatives: *Do* you *walk* regularly? Yes, I *do* (*walk*). *Does* she *care* for him? Yes, she *does* (*care*). *Do* the students *like* Dr. Blank? They *do* (*like* him). I *do* not (*don*'t) *walk*. She *does* not (*doesn*'t) *care* for him. The students *do* not (*don*'t) *like* Dr. Blank. Use this form also when you want to emphasize the verb: You never remember my birthday. Yes, I *do remember* it.

(2) The past tense
- **The basic past form** (using the second principal part). Note the *-ed* ending (on regular verbs only):

	Singular	Plural
First person	I walk**ed** [regular], I saw [irregular]	we walk**ed**, saw
Second person	you walk**ed**, saw	you walk**ed**, saw
Third person	he/she/it walk**ed**, saw	they walk**ed**, saw

Use this form for an action that was completed at a definite time in the past, or done regularly and completed in the past: I *walked* two miles yesterday. I *attended* college for two years.

- **The past progressive form:**

	Singular	Plural
First person	I was walk**ing**	we were walk**ing**
Second person	you were walk**ing**	you were walk**ing**
Third person	he/she/it was walk**ing**	they were walk**ing**

Use this form to stress that something was in progress at a time in the past: I *was walking* last night. She *was studying* when I called her. Use the past progressive also in questions (and their answers) and negatives as follows: *Were* you *walking*? *Was* she *walking*? *Were* the Smiths *coming*? I *was* not (*wasn*'t) *walking*. She *was* not (*wasn*'t) *walking*. The Smiths *were* not (*weren*'t) *coming*.

- **The past emphatic form:**

	Singular	Plural
First person	I did walk	we did walk
Second person	you did walk	you did walk
Third person	he/she/it did walk	they did walk

Use this form in most other questions (and their answers) and to emphasize an action: *Did* you *walk* [yesterday or regularly]? Yes, I *did* (*walk*). *Did* she *care* for him? Yes she *did* (*care*). *Did* the students *like* Dr. Blank? They *did* (*like* him). I *did* not (*didn*'t) *walk*. She *did* not (*didn*'t) *care* for him. The students *did* not (*didn*'t) *like* Dr. Blank. Yes, I *did remember* your birthday.

(3) The future tense
- **The basic form** (*shall* or *will* + the first principal part):

  Note: In Canada, *I shall* and *we shall* are considered very formal. *Shall,* everywhere, in all persons, also conveys determination or command: We *shall overcome*. They *shall* not *pass*.

	Singular	Plural
First person	I will/shall walk	we will/shall walk
Second person	you will walk	you will walk
Third person	he/she/it will walk	they will walk

Use this form for future happenings: I *will* (*shall*) *walk* tomorrow. She *will study* just before the test. The Smiths *will come*. *Will* you *walk* tomorrow? I *will* (*walk*). I'*ll walk*.

- **The future progressive form:**

	Singular	Plural
First person	I will/shall be walking	we will/shall be walking
Second person	you will be walking	you will be walking
Third person	he/she/it will be walking	they will be walking

Use this form to stress that something will be in progress: I *will* (I'*ll*) *be leaving* soon. She *will* (She'*ll*) *be studying* when you call. *Will* she *be studying*? No, she *will* not (*won*'t) *be studying*.

There is no emphatic form for the future or any of the following tenses.

(4) The present perfect tense
- **The basic form** (*have* or *has* + the third principal part):

	Singular	Plural
First person	I have walk**ed**, I have seen	we have walk**ed**, seen
Second person	you have walk**ed**, seen	you have walk**ed**, seen
Third person	he/she/it has walk**ed**, seen	they have walk**ed**, seen

Use this form generally when something happened in the past but has some connection with the present, or was completed at some indefinite time in the past: I *have (I've) walked* for hours. She *has (She's) studied* since midnight. Ms. Stein *has lived* here 40 years [lived here in the past, still lives here]. He *has received* constant death threats [began in the past, may still be going on]. They *have signed* a contract [at some indefinite time in the past].

- **The progressive present perfect:** I *have been walking*, she *has been walking*, and so forth. Use this form to stress that something has been and still is in progress: I *have (I've) been walking* since noon. *Have* you *been walking*? I *have* not (*haven't*) been *walking*.

(5) The past perfect tense

- **The basic past perfect form** (*had* + the third principal part):

	Singular	Plural
First person	I had walk**ed**	we had walk**ed**
Second person	you had walk**ed**	you had walk**ed**
Third person	he/she/it had walk**ed**	they had walk**ed**

Use this form for something completed earlier than, or up to the time of, something else in the past: I *had walked* for hours before help came. Until I arrived with the car, she *had walked*. The witness said [yesterday] that she *had seen* the accident [last month]. She *had lived* there 40 years when the building collapsed.

- **The progressive past perfect form:** I *had been walking*, she *had been walking*, and so forth. Use this form to stress that something was in progress earlier than, or up to the time of, something else in the past: I *had been investing* heavily when the market collapsed. She *had been acting* depressed before her suicide.

(6) The future perfect tense

- **The basic future perfect form** (*shall* or *will have* + the third principal part):

	Singular	Plural
First person	I will/shall have walk**ed**	we will/shall have walk**ed**
Second person	you will have walk**ed**	you will have walk**ed**
Third person	he/she/it will have walk**ed**	they will have walk**ed**

Use this form for something that will already be completed at a certain future time: I *shall/will have walked* five miles by the time I get home. They *will have left* when you reach their home. By March [future time] Stark *will* already *have left* office [completed action]. When I reach Winnipeg [future], she *will have found* my letter [completed action]. (Note that future event, *reach,* uses the present tense.)

- **The progressive future perfect form:** I *shall/will have been walking*, she *will have been walking*, and so forth. Use this form to stress that something will have been in progress: By midnight she *will have been studying* for fifteen hours nonstop. Next Monday he *will have been working* here a month.

  Note: Sometimes there seems little difference in meaning between the basic and progressive perfect forms, and either will do: I *have waited* here since noon. I *have been waiting* here since noon.

(7) The conditional forms. Use the conditional forms (I *would walk*, you *would walk*, and so forth; I *would have walked*, you *would have walked*, he *would have walked*, and so forth) when something depends on some less-than-probable condition. Use *would* for a future condition: If the stock market rose [in the future], bond prices *would fall*. (Note that the other verb, *rose,* uses the past tense.) Use *would have* for a past condition that did not actually happen: If the stock market had risen [it did not], bond prices *would have fallen*. (Note that the other verb, *had risen,* uses the past perfect tense.)

Do not use *would* in both clauses:

  Wrong: If the stock market *would have risen,* bond prices *would have fallen.*

  Right: If the stock market *had risen,* bond prices *would have fallen.*

Do not use have as an auxiliary in both verbs:

  Wrong: They *would have liked* to have seen Paris.

  Right: They *would have liked* [in the past] to *see* Paris. They *would like* [now] to *have seen* Paris [in the past]. They *would like* [now] to *see* Paris [in the future].

(8) Other modals (*can, could, may, might, must, should*). See 13D, page 6.

C. Make the Verb Agree in Person and Number with the Subject. Sections 23–24, pages 17–19, deal with the very important topic of agreement.

D. Distinguish a Verbal from a Verb. A **verbal** is a form derived from a verb. It is used not as a verb but as a noun, adjective, or adverb. There are three kinds of verbals: **infinitives**, **participles**, and **gerunds**.

(1) Infinitive (*to* + verb), used as

- Noun:

    To act is her ambition. [subject]

    She desires *to act.* [direct object]

    Her ambition is *to act.* [subjective complement]

- Adjective:

    Hers is an ambition *to admire.* [modifies *ambition*]

- Adverb:

    Her goal is not easy *to attain.* [modifies *easy*]

    She came here *to study.* [modifies *came*]

(2) Participle, used as adjective:

- Present participle (verb + *-ing*):

    The *cheering* crowd stormed the stage. [modifies *crowd*]

    The crowd, *cheering* wildly, stormed the stage. [modifies *crowd*]

- Past participle (third principal part of verb: for regular verbs, verb + *-ed*; for irregular verbs, no set form but often ends in *-en*):

    Confused students wandered the campus. [modifies *students*]

    Completely *confused,* students wandered the campus. [modifies *students*]

    The economy, *driven* by consumer demand, kept expanding. [modifies *economy*]

Use the *present participle* with a person or thing that is doing something: a *devastating* flood (the flood is doing the devastating). Use the *past participle* with a person or thing to which something has been done: the *devastated* land (the land has had devastation done to it).

(3) Gerund (verb + *-ing*), used as noun:

    Seeing [subject] is *believing* [subjective complement].

    The prisoners considered *escaping* [direct object] by *tunnelling* [object of preposition].

See 40C, page 30, for possessives with gerunds.

Note: An *-ing* verbal may be either a gerund or a participle, depending on its use in a particular sentence:

Swimming is excellent exercise. [gerund: used as subject noun]

The *swimming* child reached the raft. [participle: used as adjective, modifying *child*]

Infinitives, participles, and gerunds also have a *have* form for events already past: *To have worked* so hard exhausted him [infinitive]. *Having worked* hard for years, he was glad to retire [participle]. He was praised for *having worked* so hard [gerund].

15. Avoiding Verb Errors

A. Do Not Shift Tense Without Reason.

Wrong: In the film she *becomes* pregnant but *refused* to name the father.

Right: In the film she *becomes* pregnant but *refuses* to name the father.

Right: In the film she *became* pregnant but *refused* to name the father.

B. Do Not Overuse the Passive Voice.
Transitive verbs have two voices. In the **active voice**, the more common one, the subject does the action (it is the "doer"): A million citizens rousingly *cheered* the Queen. (The subject, *citizens,* did the cheering.) In the **passive voice**, the subject "receives" the action (it is being acted upon, having the action done to it), and the doer is put inside a *by* phrase or not mentioned at all: The Queen *was cheered* rousingly by a million citizens. The Queen *was cheered* rousingly.

The passive voice uses *be* (*am, is, was . . .*) + the past participle: *was cheered, is held, might have been told, will be shot.* In general, the active voice, which stresses the doer of an action, is more forceful than the passive, which stresses the receiver. To make a passive sentence active, ask "Who is doing the action?" Make the answer your subject. In the sentences below, Margaret Atwood is doing the action—reading:

Passive: The poem *will be read* by **Margaret Atwood**.

Active: **Margaret Atwood** *will read* the poem.

But do use the passive when

- The doer is unimportant: The package *will be delivered* soon. [The deliverer's name is unimportant.]

- Your emphasis is on the receiver: The MP *has been punched* by an irate taxpayer. [The focus is on the MP, not the puncher.]

- The doer is unknown: Their car *was stolen* from the driveway.

- You want to de-emphasize or conceal the doer: Yes, an error *has been made* at this office. [The person who committed the error is not named.]

Avoid needless shifting between active and passive. See 27D(3), page 24.

C. Do Not Shift Mood Without Reason.
The mood of a verb indicates how the idea of a sentence is to be regarded. Sentences that state facts or ask questions are in the **indicative** mood:

Kinshasa *is* the capital of Zaire.

Is Kinshasa the capital of Zaire?

Requests and commands are in the **imperative mood**:

Take Flight 715 for Kinshasa. [*You* is the understood subject.]

The **subjunctive mood** expresses doubt, uncertainty, wish, or supposition or signals a condition contrary to fact. In the subjunctive mood, *am, is,* and *are* become *be; was* becomes *were; has* becomes *have;* and *-s* endings are dropped from other verbs:

> **Wish:** God *be* with you. Long *live* the Queen. Far *be* it from me [that is, *May it be far from me*] to interfere in his life.

> **Doubt or uncertainty:** If I *were* to tell him, he might tell everyone.

> **Condition contrary to fact:** If I *were* you, I would tell.

Use the subjunctive also in a *that* clause when the main clause expresses a demand, command, recommendation, request, or parliamentary motion:

> They demanded that the management *refund* their money.

> The board recommends that the treasurer *resign* at once.

> I move that the meeting *be* adjourned.

Do not shift moods illogically:

> **Wrong:** First *press* the ESC key; then you *should exit* from the program. [*Press* is imperative in mood; *should exit*, indicative.]

> **Right:** First *press* the ESC key; then *exit* from the program.

D. Do Not Misuse Irregular Verb Forms. Here are the standard principal parts of some common troublesome verbs. Asterisked verbs (*) are further treated in 83, pages 48–52.

ESL

Present Tense	Past Tense	Past Participle
[be] am, is, are	was, were	been
begin	began	begun
blow	blew	blown
*break	broke	broken
*bring	brought	brought
choose	chose	chosen
(be)come	(be)came	(be)come
cost	cost	cost
do	did	done
drink	drank	drunk
drive	drove	driven
fall	fell	fallen
fly	flew	flown
forbid	forbade, forbad	forbidden

Present Tense	Past Tense	Past Participle
freeze	froze	frozen
give	gave	given
go	went	gone
grow	grew	grown
know	knew	known
*lay [to put]	laid	laid
*lead	led	led
*lie [to rest]	lay	lain
*lose	lost	lost
mean	meant	meant
pay	paid	paid
read [say "reed"]	read [say "red"]	read [say "red"]
ride	rode	ridden
ring	rang	rung
*(a)rise	(a)rose	(a)risen
run	ran	run
say	said	said
see	saw	seen
seek	sought	sought
shake	shook	shaken
shine [to give off light]	shone	shone

[*Shine*—to polish—is a different verb. It is regular.]

Present Tense	Past Tense	Past Participle
show	showed	shown, showed
sink	sank	sunk
speak	spoke	spoken
steal	stole	stolen
swear	swore	sworn
swim	swam	swum
swing	swung	swung
*take	took	taken
tear	tore	torn
think	thought	thought
throw	threw	thrown
(a)wake	(a)woke, (a)waked	(a)waked, (a)woke(n)

[*Awaken* is a different verb. It is regular.]

wear	wore	worn
*write	wrote	written

E. Do Not Confuse Verbs Similar in Meaning or Spelling. Sometimes mentally substituting a synonym for the verb that is puzzling you (such as *rest* for *lie* and *put* for *lay*) helps solve your puzzle. Many sets of troublesome verbs, such as *lie/lay* and *affect/effect* are explained in 83, pages 48–52.

16–17. Using Adjectives and Adverbs

Recall that an adjective modifies (describes or limits) a noun or occasionally a pronoun, and that an adverb modifies a verb or sometimes another modifier (adjective or adverb):

> **Adjectives:** [descriptive] a *red* barn, a *swift* ride, a *happy* man; [limiting] *this* isle, *seven* clowns, *some* cookies.

> **Adverbs:** The horse ran *swiftly*. [modifying a verb, *ran*] The horse was *very* swift. [modifying an adjective, *swift*] The horse ran *very* swiftly. [modifying an adverb, *swiftly*]

Many adverbs are formed by the addition of *-ly* to adjectives:

> smooth → smoothly   regrettable → regrettably
> delightful → delightfully easy → easily

An *-ly* ending thus usually signals an adverb—but not always, for *friendly, womanly,* and *saintly* are adjectives. A few common adverbs have the same form as their corresponding adjectives: *late, early, fast.* Some adverbs have two forms: *slow(ly), quick(ly).* The sure way to tell an adjective from an adverb is to determine the word that is modified: You drive too *fast* [drive how? *fast:* adverb]. You are in the *fast* lane [which lane? *fast:* adjective].

The word *not* is an adverb.

16. Using Adjectives and Adverbs Correctly

A. Use an Adverb, Not an Adjective,

(1) To modify an action verb:

> **Wrong:** The team played *careless* today.
> **Right:** The team played *carelessly* today.

(2) To modify an adjective:

> **Wrong:** This was a *real* good game.
> **Right:** This was a *really* good game.

(3) To modify another adverb:

> **Wrong:** Tamara tries *awful* hard.
> **Right:** Tamara tries *awfully* (better, *extremely*) hard.

B. Use an Adjective (as Subjective Complement) After a Linking Verb.

> The weather was *dismal*. [*Dismal* describes *weather*.]
> Our tiny room smelled *damp*. [*Damp* describes *room*.]

See 13C, pages 5–6, for an explanation and full list of linking verbs and an example of the same verb as both linking and action.

C. Use *Good* and *Well, Bad* and *Badly* Correctly. **Use good and bad (adjectives) as complements after a linking verb: This is good. I feel good. This fish tastes bad.** Use *well* and *badly* (adverbs) to modify an action verb: She sings *well*. I have failed *badly*.

> **Note:** *Well* can be an adjective in the limited sense of "in good health": I am feeling *well*. She is not a *well* woman. *I feel good,* on the other hand, refers to any kind of good feeling.

D. Use Comparative and Superlative Forms Correctly.

(1) Most adjectives and adverbs have three degrees. Notice how the -er and -est endings change the degree:

> **Positive (modifying one thing or action):** The Toyonda is a *sleek* car that can accelerate *fast*.

> **Comparative (comparing two):** The Chrysillac is the *sleeker* of the two cars, and it can accelerate *faster*.

> **Superlative (comparing three or more):** The Lexwagen is the *sleekest* car on the road, and it can accelerate (the) *fastest* of all.

Most long adjectives and most adverbs use *more* and *most* instead of -er and -est: *fanciful, more fanciful, most fanciful; smoothly, more smoothly, most smoothly.* Some adjectives and adverbs use either form: *costlier, costliest or more costly, most costly.* (To express the opposite of *more* and *most,* use *less* and *least: less smoothly, least smoothly.*)

(2) A few adjectives and adverbs have irregular forms of comparison:

> good/well, better, best   many/much, more, most
> bad/badly, worse, worst   little, less, least

(3) Use the comparative (not the superlative) when comparing two things:

> **Wrong:** Lee is the *smallest* of the twins.
> **Right:** Lee is the *smaller* of the twins.

E. Use Articles and Determiners Correctly. `ESL`

(1) A *and* an. Before a vowel sound (*a, e, i, o, u,* sometimes *y*) use *an: an* accident, *an* image, *an* honest person (*h* is silent), *an* uncle, *an* MP (em-pee), *an* $80 (eighty-dollar) cheque. Before a consonant (any non-vowel) sound, use *a: a* car, *a* mystery, *a* hotel (*h* is pronounced), *a* university (*u* pronounced as consonant *yu*), a *D* (dee), *a* $70 (seventy-dollar) cheque.

(2) Count and non-count nouns. A **count noun** is one that can be counted, such as *car:* one car, two cars, three cars, several cars . . .; one reason, two reasons, many reasons. . . . A **non-count noun** cannot be counted: *health* (we do not say *one health, two healths, many healths*), *courage, gold*. Non-count nouns include concepts and qualities *(truth, honesty)*, emotions *(sadness)*, activities *(swimming)*, substances *(methane, milk)*, school subjects *(chemistry)*, and other non-countables *(baggage, underwear)*. Certain nouns are sometimes non-count (I felt *joy*) and sometimes count (the *joys* of youth).

A **familiar term** is one that we already know; the writer may have mentioned it already or may explain it immediately, or it may be in our prior knowledge (such as your campus gym). An **unfamiliar** term is the opposite: the writer has not previously mentioned it or does not immediately explain it, nor is it in our prior knowledge (a faraway gym, any gym).

Use articles (*a, an, the*) as follows:

Before—	Use—	Example
COUNT NOUNS Unfamiliar singular	*a* or *an*	*An* [any] accident *victim* needs *a* [any] good *lawyer. A* bus has skidded into *a* tree. [Reader has not known about the bus or tree before.]
Unfamiliar plural	[no article]	*Fires* broke out in Alberta. [Reader has not known of these before.] *Victims* [any victims] need *lawyers* promptly.
Familiar (singular or plural)	*the*	[Victim and lawyer mentioned in previous sentence.] *The victim* should see *the lawyer* promptly. *The war* is over. *The stars* are out.
NON-COUNT NOUN	[usually no article]	*Peace* is near. She prefers *wine*. They fought with *honour*.

Other uses of articles:

Before—	Use—	Example
SUPERLATIVES	*the*	*the most fearful child, the highest ratings*
PROPER NOUNS singular	[mostly no article]	*Australia, Lake Erie, Vanier College, Queen Victoria* BUT: *the Titanic, the Nile, the Red Sea, the University of Guelph, the Senate, the Sphinx*
plural	*the*	*the Great Lakes, the Smiths, the Argonauts*

Use limiting adjectives (determiners) as follows:

Before—	Use (with example)—
COUNT NOUNS singular	*one* day, *every* way, *each* new clerk, *either* person, *another* problem
plural	*many* flights, *most* days, *(a) few* new ideas *all* (the) cars, *other* people, *such* hats, *both* nations, *enough* apples, *some* players, *more* people
NON-COUNT NOUNS	*most* rain, *all* traffic, *other* equipment, *such* joy, *more* noise, *enough* trouble, *(a) little* time, *some* sugar

For more on determiners, see 6A, page 2.

(3) *Order of adjectives*. Before a noun, place adjectives in this order, from the beginning:

1. Articles, determiners, and possessive nouns or pronouns: *the, some, my, Janet's* (my friends)

2. Numbers: *five, fifth* (my five friends)

3. Descriptive adjectives: *enormous, round, old, silver, cranky* (my five old friends)

4. Nouns used as adjectives: *car* wheels, *bank* loans, *elephant* tusks (my five old college friends)

For more on modifiers, see Section 27, pages 22–24.

17. Avoiding Adjective and Adverb Errors

A. Do Not Use Both Forms of the Comparative (*-er* and *More*) or of the Superlative (*-est* and *Most*) Together.

One form is enough:

> **Wrong:** This beam is *more stronger* than the other.
>
> **Right:** This beam is *stronger* than the other.
>
> **Wrong:** She is the *most unlikeliest* of heroes.
>
> **Right:** She is the *unlikeliest* (or the *most unlikely*) of heroes.

B. Do Not Compare Adjectives That Cannot Logically Be Compared, such as *unique, fatal, impossible, square, empty*. A task is either possible or impossible; it cannot be more (or less) impossible. Instead, say *more nearly impossible*.

> **Wrong:** Newman's diagram is *more square* than Lombardo's. [A *square* must have four 90° angles; *more or less* square is not possible.]
>
> **Right:** Newman's diagram is *more nearly square* than Lombardo's.

For more information on adjectives and adverbs see Sections 27A(2), (3), pages 22–23, and 27B, pages 23–24.

18–20. Using Pronouns

A pronoun substitutes for a noun, so that instead of saying *The song was so popular for the song's witty lyrics that the song sold a million copies,* we can say *The song was so popular for its witty lyrics that it sold a million copies.* The noun that the pronoun substitutes for (stands for) is called its **antecedent**. In the sentence above, *Song* is the antecedent of *its* and *it.* (Not all kinds of pronouns have expressed antecedents.)

Pronouns share almost all the uses of nouns. (To review those uses, see 11, pages 4–5.)

18. The Kinds of Pronouns

A. The Personal Pronouns. These designate one or more particular persons or things:

Person	Singular	Plural
FIRST [person(s) speaking]	I, my, mine, me	we, our, ours, us
SECOND [person(s) spoken to]	you, your, yours	you, your, yours
THIRD [any other person(s) or thing(s)]	he, his, him, she, her, hers. it, its	they, their, theirs, them

B. The Interrogative and Relative Pronouns

(1) The interrogative pronouns are *who (whose, whom), which, what.* They ask questions:

> *Who* broke the silence? *Whose* voice was heard? *What* was said? *Which* of the members spoke? To *whom* was the remark directed?

(2) The relative pronouns are the same as the interrogative, plus *that* and the *-ever* forms: *whoever (whomever), whichever, whatever.* Relative pronouns introduce certain kinds of dependent clauses (sometimes called **relative clauses**):

> The diplomat *who spied* was arrested.
> VCRs, *which are quite complex,* puzzle me.
> The Prime Minister will announce *whatever* Cabinet decides.

Use *who* for persons, *which* for things, and *that* for either:

> **Person:** Students *who* (or *that*) use the dining hall must have meal cards.
> **Thing:** Tonight's meal is pizza, *which* I enjoy. A meal *that* I enjoy is pizza.

Note: When *of which* sounds awkward, you may use *whose* with things: Venice is a city *whose* traffic jams are confined to waterways.

C. The Demonstrative Pronouns are *this* (plural: *these*) and *that* (plural: *those*). They point out:

> *This* is the page. Take any one of these.
> *That* is her office. Those are the elevators.

D. The Indefinite Pronouns refer to no particular person or thing:

Number	Indefinite Pronouns
Singular	another, anybody, anyone, anything, each, either, everybody, everyone, everything, neither, nobody, no one, nothing, one, somebody, someone, something
Plural	both, few, many, others, several
Singular or Plural	all, any, more, most, none, some, such

> *Many* will complain, but *few* will act; *most* will do *nothing.*
> *Someone* must do *something,* but *no one* wants to do *anything.*

Note: Closely related to the indefinite pronouns are the two **reciprocal** pronouns, *each other* and *one another.* See 83, pages 48–52.

E. The Reflexive and Intensive Pronouns are the *-self* forms of personal pronouns: *myself, yourself, yourselves, himself, herself, itself, ourselves, themselves.*

(1) They are called reflexive when used as objects or as subjective complements:

> The computer will reboot *itself* after a shutdown [direct object]. The students produced the yearbook by *themselves* [object of preposition]. The dean is not *herself* today [subjective complement].

(2) They are called intensive when used as appositives, for emphasis:

> I *myself* am to blame. Only they *themselves* are to blame.

Do not use a *-self* pronoun where a personal pronoun suffices:

> **Wrong:** The message was for Pat and *myself.*
> **Right:** The message was for Pat and *me.*

Note: There are no such words in standard English as *hisself, ourselfs, theirself, theirselves, yourselfs, themself, themselfs.*

19. Using the Right Case.
The case of a pronoun is the form it takes in a particular use in a sentence (subject, direct object, etc.). English has three cases: **nominative**, **possessive**, and **objective**.

	Nominative Case (subject forms)	Possessive Case (possessive forms)	Objective Case (object forms)
Singular	I	my, mine	me
	he, she, it	his, her, hers, its	him, her, it
Plural	we	our, ours	us
	they	their, theirs	them
Singular and Plural	you	your, yours	you
	who	whose	whom

The pronouns with different nominative and objective forms cause the most confusion: *I/me, he/him, she/her, we/us, they/them, who/whom.*

A. Nominative Case. Use the distinctive nominative (subject) forms—*I, he, she, we, they, who*—for

(1) Subject: *I* know it. *He* and *I* know it. *Who* knows it? *They* know it.

(2) Subjective complement (after linking verbs): The only one invited was *she.*

> *Note:* Although *It was her* or *It wasn't me* is common in informal usage, most writers and speakers adhere to the nominative in formal usage: It was *she.* It was not *I.* If a sentence such as *The only one invited was she* sounds awkward, you can recast it: *She was the only one invited.* See C(4) note below for pronoun case with the infinitive *to be.*

B. Objective Case. Use the distinctive object(ive) forms—*me, him, her, us, them, whom*—for any kind of object:

> **Direct object:** The environmentalists castigated *him.*
> **Indirect object:** He told *her* and *me* the details.
> **Object of preposition:** He told the details to *us.*

C. Special Problems with Nominative and Objective Cases. (For who and whom, see D and E below.)

(1) A pronoun in a compound (with *and, or, but*) takes the same case as it would if not compounded:

> **Wrong:** *Him* and *me* can go. [Would you say *Him* can go or *Me* can go?]
> **Right:** *He* and *I* can go. [*He* can go. *I* can go.]
> **Wrong:** Awards went to Sam and *I.* [to *I?*]
> **Right:** Awards went to Sam and *me.* [to *me*]

Note: Sam and myself is also wrong. See 18E(2), page 13.

> **Wrong:** Between you and *I* there should be no secrets.
> **Right:** Between you and *me* there should be no secrets.

(2) A pronoun followed by a noun appositive takes the same case as it would without the noun:

> **Wrong:** Only *us* Torontonians know. [*us* know?]
> **Right:** Only *we* Torontonians know. [*we* know]
> **Right:** It is known only to *us* Torontonians. [to *us*]

For definition of *appositive,* see 11D, page 5.

(3) A pronoun appositive takes the same case as the word to which it is in apposition:

> Two *students, you* and *she,* will share the prize.
> Professor Hunt told *us*—Len and *me*—to leave.
> Let's [Let *us*] *you* and *me* try the bookstore.

(4) A pronoun in an incomplete comparison takes the same case as if the comparison were complete:

> **Right:** She liked Pat more than *I* [did].
> **Right:** She liked Pat more than [she liked] *me.*

Note: A pronoun between a verb and an infinitive (called the **subject of the infinitive**) takes the objective case: They urged *her* to run. She asked *them* to reconsider. If the infinitive *to be* has such a subject, any pronoun following *to be* takes the same case as the subject of the sentence (nominative): The winner was thought to be *she.*

D. *Who* and *Whom* as Interrogative Pronouns. *Who* is nominative case; *whom* is objective:

> *Who* voted against the child-support law? [subject]
> *Whom* can the people blame? → The people can blame *whom?* [direct object]
> *Whom* can people appeal to? → To *whom* can people appeal? [object of preposition]

Note: When in doubt about using *who* or *whom,* try substituting *he* or *him.* If *he* sounds right, use *who;* if *him* sounds right, use *whom:*

> (Who/Whom) rang the bell? → *He* rang the bell. *Who* rang the bell?
> (Who/Whom) did you see? → You did see *him.* → You did see *whom?* → *Whom* did you see?

Although *Who did you see?* and *Who did you go with?* are common in informal usage, *whom* is expected in formal usage. Directly after a preposition, always use *whom:* With *whom* did you go? (Exception—when the subject of a noun clause follows the preposition: Canada sent arms to *whoever fought Hitler* [not *whomever*—see E below]).

E. *Who* and *Whom* as Relative Pronouns. The case of a relative pronoun is determined by its use *within* its clause:

> Liu is the one **who** arranged the affair. [Who = subject of *arranged.*]
> Liu is the one **whom** we should thank. [→ *we should thank whom.* Whom = direct object of *should thank.*]
> We should also thank **whoever** helped her. [Whoever = subject of *helped.*]

We should inform **whomever** *we see.* [→ *we see whomever. Whomever* = direct object of *see.*]

Send a note to **whoever** *participated in the affair.* [*Whoever* = subject of *participated.*]

Do not be misled by other intervening clauses, such as *I think, it seems,* or *we are convinced:*

Liu is the one **who** ☐ I think ☐ *arranged the affair.*

Liu is the one **whom** ☐ it seems ☐ *we should thank.*

F. Possessive Case

(1) Use the apostrophe ['] to form the possessive case of indefinite and reciprocal pronouns: *someone's, everybody's, no one's, each other's, etc.*

(2) Use the possessive case before a gerund:

> **Wrong:** We resented him leaving.

> **Right:** We resented his leaving.

(3) Do not use the apostrophe in the possessive case of personal pronouns (his, hers, its, ours, yours, theirs) or of who (whose): *Whose* book is this? Is it *ours* or *theirs?* It can't be *hers.* It is a common error to confuse the possessives *its, whose, their,* and *your* with the contractions *it's, who's, they're,* and *you're.*

Possessive Pronouns (never take apostrophe)	Contractions (always take apostrophe)
its	it's (it is)
their	they're (they are)
your	you're (you are)
whose	who's (who is)

> The store lost *its* licence. *Whose* fault was that?

> The stores lost *their* licences. Was *your* store included?

Note: To tell which form you need, mentally substitute the uncontracted form (*it is,* etc.). If it sounds right, you need the contraction:

> *(Its/It's)* a fine day → *It is* a fine day → *It's* a fine day. The tree shed *(its/it's)* leaves → The tree shed *it is* leaves? → No. The tree shed *its* leaves.

20. Avoiding Faulty Reference.
Be sure that each pronoun refers unmistakably only to its antecedent—the noun it stands for.

A. Ambiguous Reference occurs when a pronoun may refer to more than one noun. Clarify such ambiguity by rephrasing the sentence:

> **Ambiguous:** This program will not work on a model 5X computer because *it* is too old. [Does *it* refer to the program or the computer?]

> **Clear:** This program will not work on a model 5X computer, *which* is too old.

> **Clear:** This program, *which* is too old, will not work on a model 5X computer.

B. Vague Reference occurs when a pronoun has no easily identifiable antecedent. Clarify the sentence by supplying the needed noun:

> **Vague:** In Japan *they* name *their* years after animals. [*They* and *their* have no antecedent. Who are *they?*]

> **Clear:** The *Japanese* name their years after animals.

Avoid using *which, it, this,* or *that* to refer to a whole clause or sentence in a unclear way:

> **Vague:** The treaty was approved by Parliament, *which* raised hopes for world peace. [Can you find a clear antecedent for *which? Parliament?* The *treaty?* Actually, neither. It is the *approval.*]

> **Clear:** The treaty's *approval* by Parliament raised hopes for world peace.

> **Vague:** Acid rain is still a problem in Ontario, thus increasing support for a stronger anti-pollution law in Parliament. What will happen because of *this* is uncertain.

> **Clear:** . . . What will happen because of *this new support* is uncertain.

> **Clear:** . . . What will happen because of *this continued pollution* is uncertain.

Note: A possessive noun cannot logically be the antecedent of a nominative or objective pronoun:

> **Wrong:** Princess *Diana's* death stunned the world, for *she* had been loved by millions. [*She* cannot have a possessive, *Diana's,* as antecedent.]

> **Right:** Diana's death stunned the world, for the *princess* had been loved by millions.

It is acceptable in *It is raining, It is a fine day,* and so on.

21–22. Recognizing Phrases and Clauses

Being able to recognize phrases and clauses helps you avoid agreement errors, fragments, comma splices, fused sentences, and misplaced or dangling modifiers.

21. Phrases.
A *phrase* is a group of related words that is less than a sentence because it lacks subject + verb. (Some phrases contain a part of a verb—a verbal.) A phrase usually functions as if it were a single word: noun, adjective, or adverb. For this reason it is important to think of and recognize phrases as units. There are two main kinds of phrases.

A. The Prepositional Phrase is used chiefly as an adjective or adverb. It consists of preposition + object (and possible modifiers of that object):

> **As adjective:** The CD player *with the best sound* is lowest in price. [tells which player]
>
> **As adverb:** I bought it *at a discount store*. [tells where] I bought it *for a birthday gift*. [tells why]

See 7B, pages 3–4, for a list of prepositions.

B. The Verbal Phrase. There are three kinds: infinitive, participial, and gerund. (See 14D, pages 8–9, for explanation of these terms).

(1) An infinitive phrase (infinitive + complement or modifiers or both):

> **As noun:** *To become premier* is her aim. [subject]
>
> She wants *to become premier*. [direct object]
>
> **As adjective:** I have a plan *to suggest to you*. [modifies *plan*]
>
> **As adverb:** We sued the company *to obtain justice*. [modifies *sued*]
>
> Darryl is eager *to leave soon*. [modifies *eager*]

(2) A participial phrase (present or past participle + complement or modifiers or both). It is always used as an adjective:

> A computer *using a modem* can access the Internet. [modifies *computer*]
>
> *Equipped with a modem*, a computer can access the Internet. [modifies *computer*]

Another kind of phrase using a participle is the **absolute phrase** (subject + participle + possible complement or modifiers or both), so called because it is grammatically independent of the sentence (though logically connected to it):

> *Her heart pounding*, Karen rose to speak.
>
> Karen rose to speak, *her heart pounding*.

(3) A gerund phrase (*-ing* form + complement or modifiers or both). It is always used as a noun:

> *Saving the environment* will take worldwide effort. [subject]
>
> The speaker stressed *saving the environment*. [direct object]
>
> What can we do about *saving the environment?* [object of preposition]
>
> Her chief concern is *saving the environment*. [subjective complement]

For avoidance of misplaced or dangling phrases, see 27A(2), (3), B, pages 22–24.

Note: Some authorities use the term **noun phrase** to refer to a noun and its modifiers *(the five old men in their wheelchairs)*, and **verb phrase** for a main verb and its auxiliaries *(might have been drinking)*.

22. Clauses. A *clause* is a group of related words containing subject + verb. There are two kinds: *independent (main)* and *dependent (subordinate)*.

A. Kinds of Clauses

(1) An independent clause sounds complete and makes sense when it stands alone. Every simple sentence is an independent clause; however, the term *clause* usually refers to such a word group as part of a larger sentence:

> [clauses in *italics*]
>
> *The virus began to spread*, and *doctors grew alarmed*.

Independent clauses are normally connected by *and, but, yet, or, nor, for,* or *so* (coordinating conjunctions) or a semicolon(;). The conjunction is not considered part of either clause.

(2) A dependent clause, though it contains subject + verb, cannot stand alone grammatically. What makes a clause dependent is a connecting word that forces the clause to be linked to an independent clause:

> [dependent clause in italics; connecting word in **bold**]
>
> You may graduate **when** you pay your library fines.
>
> The topic **that** Elva chose was controversial.

In dependent clauses (unlike independent clauses) the connecting word is considered part of the clause.

B. Kinds of Dependent Clauses

(1) An adjective clause is used as an adjective, modifying a preceding noun or pronoun. It is introduced and connected to the independent clause by the relative pronoun *who (whose, whom), which,* or *that,* or sometimes by *when, where,* or *why:*

> Nations *that reduce tariffs* often prosper. [modifies *Nations*]
>
> It frightened everyone *who saw it*. [modifies *everyone*]
>
> Osgood's, *which is downtown*, sells CDs. [modifies *Osgood's*]
>
> That was a time *when peace prevailed*. [modifies *time*]

Sometimes you may omit the relative pronoun: The people [*that/whom*] we met were friendly. But such omission may sometimes damage clarity or tone. It is better to keep the pronoun in most formal writing situations.

Adjective clauses are either **restrictive** or **nonrestrictive**, depending on their necessity in the sentence. See 30F(1), page 26, for explanation and punctuation.

(2) *An adverb clause* is used as an adverb, modifying a verb, adjective, or other adverb. It tells *how, when, where, why, with what result, under* or *despite what condition,* or *to what degree.* It is introduced and connected to the independent clause by a subordinating conjunction, such as the ones listed below:

Adverb Clause Telling	Introduced by Subordinating Conjunction	Example
Time [*when?*]	when (ever), while, after, before, since, as, as soon as, until	They kept dancing *after the music stopped.*
Place [*where?*]	where, wherever	We went *where the land was fertile.*
Manner [*how?*]	as, as if, as though	He walks *as if he's dazed.*
Cause [*why?*]	because, since	I left *because I was angry.*
Purpose [*why?*]	(so) that, in order that	She came *so that she might help.*
Concession [*despite what condition?*]	(al)though, even though	They played, *although they were tired.*
Condition [*under what condition?*]	if, unless, whether, provided	You may go *if you leave early.*
Result [*that what resulted?*]	that	He ran so fast *that he was exhausted.*
Comparison [*to what degree?*]	as, than	She is taller *than I [am].*

You can shift most adverb clauses to the beginning of the sentence for variety, emphasis, or clarity of sequence:

> *Although they were tired,* they played.

> *If you leave early,* you may go.

(3) *A noun clause* is used as a noun. It is introduced and connected to the independent clause by the relative pronoun *who(ever), which(ever), what(ever),* or *that* or by *when, where, why, how,* or *whether*:

> *What they knew* frightened him. [subject]

> I understand *that you need help.* [direct object]

> She gave *whoever passed by* a brochure. [indirect object]

> She gave a brochure to *whoever passed by.* [object of preposition]

As with adjective clauses, you may sometimes omit *that* (I understand [*that*] you need help), but in formal writing it is usually better to keep it.

C. Clauses in Sentences. Sentences can be classified according to their structure—that is, the number and kind(s) of clauses they have. There are four kinds of sentences:

(1) *The simple sentence* (one independent clause):

> *Management made a new offer.*

(2) *The compound sentence* (two or more independent clauses):

> *Management made a new offer,* and *the union agreed.*

> *Management made a new offer, the union agreed,* and *the workers ended their strike.*

(3) *The complex sentence* (one independent clause + one or more dependent clauses):

> [dependent clause in **bold**]
> **When management made a new offer,** the union agreed.

(4) *The compound-complex sentence* (a compound sentence + one or more dependent clauses):

> **When management made a new offer,** the union agreed, and the workers ended their strike.

23–24. Agreement

In sentences, subjects and verbs have matching forms to show their grammatical relation. So do pronouns and their antecedents. This relation is called **agreement**.

23. Subject-Verb Agreement

A. Agreement in Person. Use the verb form that matches the person of the subject. (See 14B, pages 6–8, for explanation of *person.*) In most verbs, only the third person present tense singular, with the ending *-s,* causes a problem. *I run, we run,* and *you run,* but *he/she/it runs.* The verb *be* is special. The first person is *I am, we are* (past tense: *I was, we were*); the second person is *you are* (past tense: *you were*); the third person is *he/she/it is, they are* (past tense: *he/she/it was, they were*):

> ***Wrong:*** *You is* late. ***Right:*** *You* **are** late.

Note: When two or more subjects in different persons are joined by *or,* the verb agrees with the subject nearer to it: Either she or I *am* going. In a dependent clause with *who* or *that* as subject, the verb agrees with the antecedent of *who* or *that:* It is I who *am* right. [Antecedent of *who* is *I.*]

B. Agreement in Number. **Singular** number refers to one thing, and **plural** number refers to more than one. Singular subjects must take singular verbs; plural subjects must take plural verbs. Except for *be* (see A above), only the third person singular in the present causes a problem, because of its *-s* ending:

> ***Wrong:*** A *bear like* honey, but *it do*n't [*do* not] like bees.

Right: A *bear* **likes** honey, but *it* **does**n't [*does* not] like bees.

Wrong: Only one rock *concert have* been scheduled here.

Right: Only one rock *concert* **has** been scheduled here.

C. Intervening Word Groups. Make subject and verb agree regardless of phrases or clauses between them:

> **Phrase:** Their *performance* on all tests **Is** impressive.
>
> **Clause:** *Trees* that get the disease **are** cut down.

Parenthetical phrases introduced by *(together) with, like, as well as, including, in addition to,* and so on do not affect the number of the actual subject:

> The *city,* as well as the suburbs, **votes** Liberal.
>
> *Ted,* in addition to the twins, **has** accepted.

D. Two or More Subjects

(1) Joined by and: Use a plural verb:

> A *book and* a *pencil* **are** all I need.
>
> **Are** *chemistry and history* required?

However, if both subjects refer to the same single person or thing, use a singular verb:

> Her *mentor and friend* **was** at her side during the ordeal. [One person is both mentor and friend.]
>
> *Ham and eggs* **is** on the menu. [one dish]

Use a singular verb when *each* or *every* precedes the subjects:

> *Every dog and cat* **is** tested for rabies.

(2) Joined by nor or or: Make the verb agree with the nearer subject:

> *Renee or Kareem* **is** volunteering.
>
> The *Gosnells and* the *Jacksons* **are** volunteering.
>
> *Neither Renee nor the Jacksons* **are** inexperienced.
>
> *Neither the Jacksons nor Renee* **is** inexperienced.

E. Singular Pronouns. Use a singular verb when the subject is a singular indefinite pronoun, such as *one, each, either, neither, everyone, everybody, anyone, anybody, someone, somebody, no one,* or *nobody.* Do not be misled by intervening phrases or clauses:

> *Each* of the blouses in the shipments **has** a tiny defect.
>
> *Everyone* who has ever seen any of her plays **is** calling this her best.

After *all, any, most, none, some,* or *such,* use either a singular or a plural verb, depending on whether the pronoun refers to something singular or plural:

The milk was left in the sun; *all* of it **has** turned sour.

The guests became bored; *all* **have** left.

Such **were** the joys of youth. *Such* **is** the way of the world.

F. Collective Nouns. In Canadian usage, use a singular verb when thinking of the group as a unit:

> The *audience* **was** the largest this season.

Use a plural verb when thinking of the group members as individuals:

> The *audience* **were** *leaving,* one or two at a time.

G. Linking Verbs. Make a linking verb agree with its subject, not with its subjective complement:

> His *problem* **was** wild pitches. Wild *pitches* **were** his problem.

H. Singular Nouns in Plural Form. Such nouns as *news, billiards, whereabouts, athletics, measles, mumps, mathematics,* and *economics* are logically singular. Use a singular verb:

> Muller is discovering that *economics* **requires** much study.
>
> *Mumps* **leaves** some children with impaired hearing.

However, use a plural verb with two-part things such as *trousers, pants, pliers, scissors, tweezers:*

> The *tweezers* **are** not useful here; perhaps the *pliers* **are**.

I. *It* and *There* as Expletives (words with no meaning in a sentence):

(1) There *is never the subject*. In sentences beginning with *there is (was)* or *there are (were),* look *after* the verb for the subject, and make the verb agree with the subject:

> There **is** a *taxi* at the curb. [A *taxi* **is** at the curb.]
>
> There **are** two *taxis* at the curb. [Two *taxis* **are** at the curb.]
>
> There **are** a *taxi* and a *limousine* at the curb.

(2) It, *on the other hand, is always singular:*

> *It* **was** my fax machine that malfunctioned.
>
> *It* **was** our fax machines that malfunctioned.

J. Literary Titles and Words Considered as Words are always singular:

> Chaucer's *Canterbury Tales* **depicts** life in medieval England.
>
> *Zeros* **is** spelled with either *-os* or *-oes*.

K. Sums of Money and Measurements. When considering a sum as a single unit, use a singular verb:

> *Six hundred dollars* **was** too much for a guitar.

Eleven kilometres uphill **is** quite a gruelling run.

When considering individual dollars, litres, kilometres, and so on, use a plural verb:

The *loonies* **were** neatly arranged in stacks.

All those *kilometres* **take** a toll on a runner's stamina.

In an arithmetic problem, you may use either:

*Six and four **is** [**makes**] ten. Six and four **are** [**make**] ten.*

Note: *The number* takes a singular verb; *a number*, plural: *The number* of crimes **is** down. *A number* of crimes **are** unsolved.

L. Relative Pronouns. Use a singular verb if the antecedent of *who, which,* or *that* is singular; use a plural verb if the antecedent is plural:

He is the only *one* of the chimps *that* **comprehends**. [Antecedent of *that* is *one*. Only one comprehends.]

He is one of the *chimps that* **comprehend**. [Antecedent of *that* is *chimps*. Several chimps comprehend.]

24. Pronoun-Antecedent Agreement. Every pronoun must agree with its antecedent in person and number.

A. Illogical Shifts to *You*. Avoid them:

Wrong: *Students* like English 302 because it exposes *you* to classic films.

Right: *Students* like English 302 because it exposes **them** to classic films. *I* like English 302 because it exposes **me** to classic films.

B. Singular Pronouns. Generally, use a singular pronoun when referring to antecedents such as *person, woman, man, one, anyone, anybody, someone, somebody, each, either, neither, everyone, everybody:*

Neither of the nations would yield on **its** position.

Has *anyone* lost **her** bracelet?

Everyone in the fraternity pledged **his** loyalty.

A *person* should know what **he** wants in life. [or what **she** wants in life.]

For a mixed group of men and women, should you use *they* with a singular pronoun (*Everyone* lost *their* money)? In formal English, no. For discussion of this important, thorny problem, see 82A(1), page 47.

C. Antecedents Joined by *And, Or,* or *Nor*. Follow the same principles as for subject-verb agreement (see 23D, page 18).

(1) With antecedents joined by and, use a plural pronoun:

Newfoundland and British Columbia may regain **their** fisheries.

(2) With antecedents joined by or or nor, make the pronoun agree with the nearer antecedent:

Either *Newfoundland* or *British Columbia* may regain **its** industries.

Neither the *Maritimes* nor *Quebec* should see **its** wealth decline.

D. Collective Nouns. Follow the same principle as for subject-verb agreement (see 23F, page 18); let the meaning of the noun determine the number of the pronoun:

Tonight's *audience* has angered the performers by **its** rudeness.

One by one, the *audience* are leaving **their** seats.

E. Demonstrative Pronouns Used as Adjectives. Make *this, that, these,* or *those* agree with the noun it modifies:

Wrong: I like *these kind* of fish. [*These* is plural; *kind*, singular.]

Right: I like **this** *kind* of fish. I like **these** *kinds* of fish.

F. One of The . . . After *one of the*, use a plural noun:

Wrong: Vancouver is *one of the* most livable *city* in the world.

Right: Vancouver is *one of the* most livable **cities** in the world.

25–27. Effective Sentences

Effective sentences are more than just correct. Good writers edit each sentence to gain precision, clarity, economy, originality, and harmony with the rest of the paragraph.

25. Creating Effective Sentences

A. Vary Your Sentences. Sentences that plod dully along one after another, unvaried in length or structure, bore your readers and sap their attention. One short, simple sentence (*Then the net broke*) can be forceful. But a string of short sentences usually gives a choppy, juvenile effect:

The book is titled *Fifth Business*. Robertson Davies wrote it. It begins in a small Ontario town.

Strings of clauses joined by and or and so are little better:

The book is entitled *Fifth Business* and Robertson Davies wrote it, and. . . .

At the other extreme, a series of long, complex sentences can also stupefy. Like a good tennis player, vary what you serve up. See B-G below.

Vary your sentence beginnings too, where appropriate. You need not always start with the subject; try moving an adjective or adverb construction to the beginning, or shift word order for emphasis:

To attain these goals, the council met frequently.

Straining to comprehend, the family said nothing.

Such chaos they had never seen.

Caution: Do not vary just for variety's sake; you may weaken your paper, for example, by switching from active voice to passive merely for variety, or by moving a modifier to an unnatural position. Judging when and how to vary becomes easier with experience.

B. Use Coordination. You can regard related simple sentences as independent clauses and join them with a coordinating conjunction (preceded by a comma) to form a compound sentence:

> **Choppy:** Montcalm's army was small. The English hesitated to attack.
>
> **Better:** Montcalm's army was small, **but** the English hesitated to attack. [The conjunction *but* shows the contrast between the two statements.]
>
> **Choppy:** The store closed. Its clientele had moved.
>
> **Better:** The store closed, **for** its clientele had moved. [The conjunction *for* shows that one fact caused the other.]
>
> **Choppy:** French class met at noon. Art met at two.
>
> **Better:** French class met at noon, **and** art met at two. [The *and,* though it has little effect on meaning, shows that the two ideas are connected and makes a smoother-reading sentence.]

See 7A, page 3, for more on coordinating conjunctions. Avoid overuse of coordination, especially with *and* or *so*.

C. Use Compounding. Combine simple sentences that have the same subjects or verbs so that you have only one sentence, with a compound subject, verb, or other part:

> **Weak:** The Acme Company has been producing slim laptops. The Brome Company has also been producing them.
>
> **Stronger:** [**Both**] the *Acme* **and** the *Brome* companies have been producing slim laptops.
>
> **Weak:** Acme plans to distribute the laptops it makes. It will sell them too.
>
> **Stronger:** Acme plans to *distribute* **and** *sell* the laptops it makes.

D. Use Subordination. In combining simple sentences, you can emphasize one by subordinating the other—reducing it to a dependent clause. By doing so you often express the relation between ideas more clearly than by coordination or compounding. Subordinating is one of the most important skills in good writing. You may subordinate with adjective clauses, adverb clauses, or noun clauses (see 22B, pages 16–17).

(1) Adjective clauses (beginning with *who, [whose, whom], which, that, when, where*) let you show which of two ideas you consider more important. Reduce the *less* important idea to an adjective clause:

> **Weak:** They signed the treaty. This treaty banned war.
>
> **Weak:** They signed the treaty, and it banned war.

Strengthened by adjective-clause subordination:

> They signed the treaty, **which** *banned war.* [stresses the act of signing]
>
> The treaty **that** *they signed* banned war. [stresses the banning of war]

(2) Adverb clauses (beginning with *when, if, because, although*. . . . See 22B(2), page 17, for full list) let you show that two ideas are related by time, cause, condition, and the like:

> **Weak:** The lecture grew dull. Several students dozed off.

Strengthened by adverb-clause subordination:

> **When** *the lecture grew dull,* several students dozed off. [*When* stresses the time relation between the two facts.]
>
> Several students dozed off **because** *the lecture had grown dull.* [*Because* stresses the causal relation between the two facts.]

(3) Noun clauses (beginning with *who, that, what, whatever*. . . . See 22B(3), page 17, for full list) provide smoothness, conciseness, and clarity:

> **Weak:** Tickets were selling poorly. The play's backers were never told this.
>
> **Weak:** Some children are underachievers. Karp's research discovered the reasons for this problem.

Strengthened by noun-clause subordination:

> The play's backers were never told **that** *tickets were selling poorly.*
>
> Karp's research discovered **why** *some children are underachievers.*

With subordination, compounding, and coordination you can smoothly integrate three or even more ideas:

> **Weak:** Edouard Lock revolutionized Canadian dance. He introduced athletic female dancers. They roughhoused with male dancers. They even lifted and threw them around the stage.
>
> **Subordinated and coordinated:** Edouard Lock revolutionized Canadian dance **when** he introduced athletic female dancers **who** roughhoused with male dancers **and** even lifted and threw them around the stage.

Subordination can be even more effective when combined with **reduction**, explained in E below.

Caution: Do not overdo subordination; five or six clauses inexpertly combined in a sentence can bewilder readers. And never subordinate your main idea—the one you would mention if you could mention only one. See G below.

E. Use Reduction. Wherever possible, eliminate needless words by reducing clauses to phrases and phrases to single words:

> **Wordy (clause):** *Because she was discouraged about writing stories,* Erika decided to try non-fiction.
>
> **Tighter (phrase):** *Discouraged about writing stories,* Erika decided to try non-fiction.
>
> **Wordy (clause):** The person *who is holding the pistol* is the starter.
>
> **Tighter (phrase):** The person *holding the pistol* is the starter.
>
> **Wordy (phrase):** She is a child *possessed of talent.*
>
> **Tighter (word):** She is a *talented* child.

Here is the last example from D above, further tightened by reduction:

> Lock revolutionized Canadian dance by **introducing** athletic female dancers **roughhousing** with male dancers and **throwing** them around the stage.

F. Use Parallel Structure (the same grammatical form) with two or more coordinate expressions, in comparisons, and with correlative conjunctions:

> **Wrong—not parallel:**
>
> Tourists come | *to see the city's museums,* [infinitive phrase]
> | *its skyscrapers,* [noun]
> **and** | *to hear its opera company.* [infinitive phrase]
>
> **Right—parallel:**
>
> Tourists come to the city for its | *museums,* [noun]
> | *skyscrapers,* [noun]
> **and** | *opera company.* [noun]
>
> **Also parallel:**
>
> Tourists come | *to see the city's museums,*
> | *(to) gawk at its skyscrapers,*
> **and** | *(to) hear its opera company.* [all infinitive phrases]
>
> **Wrong:** The study **not only** | *examined men* verb + noun]
> | *women.* [noun]
> **but also**
>
> **Right:** The study examined **not only** | *men* [noun]
> **but also** | *women.* [noun]
>
> **Wrong:** Campers learn *scuba diving* and *to kayak.*
>
> **Right:** Campers learn *scuba diving* and *kayaking.*
>
> **Right:** Campers learn *to scuba dive* and [*to*] *kayak.*
>
> **Wrong:** The study was more *critical* than *it offered solutions.*
>
> **Right:** The study offered more *criticism* than *solutions.*

Be sure your items are parallel logically as well as grammatically:

> **Illogical:** The city has three museums, a concert hall, an opera house, and two hundred garbage

trucks. [Garbage trucks do not belong with the other items, which are cultural attractions. Avoid such illogic, unless you intend humour or irony.]

Parallelism is one of the most powerful ways to express a complex series of facts or ideas clearly.

G. Position Main Ideas Prominently. Do not bury your main point in the middle of your sentence, in a phrase or subordinate clause:

> **Poor—intended main idea** (the death of the dinosaurs) **lost in midsentence**, in a subordinate clause: Millions of years ago a huge meteorite, *which obliterated the dinosaurs,* spread a deadly cloud over the earth.

Put your main idea at the beginning or, for even more emphasis and a sense of climax, at the end.

> **Better—main point up front:** The dinosaurs were *obliterated* millions of years ago by a huge meteorite that spread a deadly cloud over the earth.
>
> **Better and climactic—main point at end:** Millions of years ago a huge meteorite, spreading a deadly cloud over the earth, *obliterated the dinosaurs.*

26. Conquering the "Big Three" Sentence Errors.
Fragments, comma splices, and fused sentences are by far the most common, and often the most obvious, of major sentence structure errors. Make it a priority to rid your papers of these faults.

A. Fragments. A fragment is a piece of a sentence, such as a phrase or dependent clause, erroneously punctuated as if it were a complete sentence. (To review information on phrases and dependent clauses see Sections 21–22, pages 15–17.) When you discover a fragment in your writing, either (1) attach the fragment to an independent clause or (2) rewrite the fragment to form a sentence by itself. Even a statement with a subject and a predicate can be a fragment if it follows a subordinating conjunction such as *if, when,* or *because,* or begins with a relative pronoun—*who(m), which, that.* In the incorrect examples below, the fragments are in *italics:*

> **Wrong:** Garbage collections decreased. *Because recycling took effect.*
>
> **Right:** Garbage collections decreased *because recycling took effect.* [fragment attached to independent clause]
>
> **Wrong:** Alex Colville's painting *Three Sheep* shows these animals as almost angelic. *Which contrasts with his portrayal of humans as fully capable of evil.*
>
> **Right:** Alex Colville's painting *Three Sheep* shows these animals as almost angelic, *which contrasts with his portrayal of humans as fully capable of evil.* [fragment attached to independent clause]
>
> **Wrong:** *An island that shimmers in the sun.*
>
> **Right:** *The island shimmers in the sun.* [fragment rewritten as a sentence by itself]

Be alert also for omitted verbs and for participial or other phrases mistakenly written as sentences:

> **Wrong:** *Her mother a maid in a rich family's house, and her father a sailor on an oil tanker.*
>
> **Right:** Her mother *was* a maid in a rich family's house, and her father *was* a sailor on an oil tanker. [verbs added to make a sentence]
>
> **Wrong:** Security was particularly tight at Dorval Airport. *Being a main entry point for smugglers. Or It being a main entry point for smugglers. Or A main entry point for smugglers.*
>
> **Right:** Security was particularly tight at Dorval Airport, *a main entry point for smugglers.*

B. Comma Splices and Fused Sentences. A comma splice is the erroneous joining of independent clauses with a comma rather than a conjunction or semicolon:

> **Wrong:** Running relieves stress, it can prolong life.
>
> **Wrong:** In recent years adults have been smoking fewer cigarettes, teenagers have been smoking more.

A **fused sentence** is the erroneous joining of independent clauses with no conjunction or punctuation at all:

> **Wrong:** Running relieves stress it can prolong life.
>
> **Wrong:** In recent years adults have been smoking fewer cigarettes teenagers have been smoking more.

To avoid such errors (both also called **run-ons**), first be sure that you can recognize an independent clause. Review 22A(1), page 16, if necessary. Next, learn these four ways to correct run-ons; choose the way that best fits your purpose and your paragraph.

(1) Separate the clauses into two sentences:

> **Right:** Running relieves stress. It can prolong life.

This is the simplest but rarely the best way, for too many short sentences make your writing sound choppy and immature. Moreover, you fail to specify a relation between the ideas in the clauses.

(2) Join the clauses with a coordinating conjunction:

> **Right:** Running relieves stress, *and* it can prolong life.

This is often a better way than making separate sentences, but you must not overuse this either. *And,* especially, shows only a very general relation between ideas.

(3) Join the clauses with a semicolon:

> **Right:** Running relieves stress; it can prolong life.

A semicolon can give your writing a formal tone; it is often effective in balanced sentences, such as *Today was delightful; yesterday was dreadful.*

(4) Join the clauses by making one of them a dependent (subordinate) clause. Join them with subordinating conjunctions, such as *because, if, when, since, after, although,* and *unless,* or with relative pronouns: *who(m), which, that.* Subordinating is often the best way to eliminate run-ons, since subordinating conjunctions and relative pronouns show the precise relation between ideas:

> **Right:** Running, which relieves stress, can prolong life.
>
> **Right:** Because running relieves stress, it can prolong life.

For more on subordination, see 22B, pages 16–17 and 25D, page 20.

Here are more corrected comma splices:

> **Wrong:** In recent years adults have been smoking fewer cigarettes, however teenagers have been smoking more.
>
> **Right:** In recent years adults have been smoking fewer cigarettes; teenagers, however, have been smoking more. [clauses joined by semicolon—see 39B, page 29]
>
> **Right:** Although adults have been smoking fewer cigarettes in recent years, teenagers have been smoking more. [first clause subordinated]
>
> **Wrong:** Cole's study (1996) concluded that pupils with more stable home environments had higher reading scores, this finding corroborated Lynch's 1987 study.
>
> **Right:** . . . higher reading scores, a finding that corroborated Lynch's 1987 study. [last clause subordinated]
>
> **Right:** . . . higher reading scores. This finding corroborated Lynch's 1987 study. [last clause made separate sentence]

27. Avoiding Other Sentence Faults

A. Needless Separation of Related Sentence Parts

(1) Do not needlessly separate subject and verb or verb and complement:

> **Awkward:** *She,* filled with dreams of happiness, *married* him.
>
> **Smooth:** Filled with dreams of happiness, *she married* him.
>
> **Awkward:** They *bought,* by emptying their bank accounts and cashing in their bonds, a large *house.*
>
> **Smooth:** By emptying their bank accounts and cashing in their bonds, they *bought* a large *house.*

(2) Place modifying words, phrases, and clauses as close as possible to the words they modify:

• Adverb:

> **Wrong:** It was sad that the cousins *almost* **lost** all their savings in the swindle. [*Almost lost* means that they came close to losing but lost nothing.]

Right: It was sad that the cousins lost *almost* **all** their savings in the swindle.

This same caution applies to *only, nearly, scarcely, hardly, just,* and *even: Only* **Sara** heard the loon, Sara *only* **heard** the loon, and Sara heard *only* the **loon** all have different meanings.

- **Phrase:**

    Wrong: *Buried a thousand feet under Yucatan,* **geologists** have found traces of a huge crater.

    Right: Geologists have found traces of a huge **crater** *buried a thousand feet under Yucatan.*

    Note: Sometimes you can correctly separate a phrase from the word it modifies, but be especially careful that no misreading is possible—that no other noun could sensibly be modified:

    Unclear: We left the outdoor party in Marty's old Volkswagen, *covered with confetti from the celebration.* [Who is covered—*we* or *Volkswagen?*]
    Clear: We left the outdoor party in an upbeat mood, *covered with confetti from the celebration.* [The phrase can sensibly refer only to *we.*]

- **Clause:**

    Wrong: Pat left the model in the **subway** *that she had built.*

    Right: Pat left in the subway the **model** *that she* had built.

For a review of information on adjectives and adverbs see 16–17, pages 11–12.

(3) Avoid "squinting" modifiers. A squinter comes between two verbs so that the reader cannot tell to which verb it refers:

    Wrong: The Alliance **vowed** *after the convention* to **unite.**

    Right: *After the convention* the Alliance **vowed** to unite.

    Right: The Alliance vowed to **unite** *after the convention.*

(4) Avoid awkward splitting of infinitives. The two parts of an infinitive belong together; avoid putting words between them (unless your sentence would otherwise be unclear or sound odd):

    Wrong: He wanted *to* every now and then *call* her.

    Right: He wanted *to call* her every now and then.

It is quite all right, however, to place an appropriate adverb within the infinitive: They decided *to quickly replace* the dog that had died.

(5) What about ending a sentence with a preposition? (They saw the house he had lived *in.*) It is now more widely accepted than in the past, but follow this rule of thumb in formal writing: Try recasting the sentence using *which*; if the result sounds smooth, not

awkward, use it: They saw the house *in which* he had lived.

    Informal: Switzerland is another country that hockey has become popular *in.*

    Formal: Switzerland is another country *in which* hockey has become popular.

Note: Some verbs contain a *particle*—a word that looks like a preposition but is actually part of the meaning of the verb—e.g., *call up, find out, give up, turn into* (become), *put up with.* It is perfectly all right—sometimes necessary—to end a formal sentence with a particle: He promised to *call* her *up.*

B. Dangling Modifiers. A modifier (usually a phrase) "dangles" when there is no word in the sentence to which it can logically or grammatically refer. Correct a dangler in any of the ways shown below.

(1) Dangling participle:

    Wrong: *Sweeping to victory in the leadership convention,* **election** seemed possible. [The nearest noun to the phrase should name the person who swept.]

    Right: *Sweeping to victory in the leadership convention,* **Day** felt hopeful of his election. [person who swept, *Day,* put nearest to phrase]

    Right: *When* **Day swept** *to victory in the leadership convention,* his election seemed possible. [phrase expanded into clause naming the person who swept]

    Note: Possessives do not count as the "nearest noun":

    Wrong: Sweeping to victory in the leadership convention, Day's **election** seemed possible.
    Right: See above.

(2) Dangling gerund:

    Wrong: *After harvesting the crops,* a **truck** hauled them to market. [Did the truck harvest the crops?]

    Right: *After harvesting the crops,* the **farmer** trucked them to market.

    Right: *After the* **farmer harvested** *the crops,* a truck hauled them to market.

(3) Dangling infinitive:

    Wrong: *To access the map program,* a floppy **disk** must be inserted. [Who is doing the accessing? Not the disk.]

    Right: *To access the map program,* **you** must insert a floppy disk. [You are doing the accessing.]

(4) Dangling elliptical clause. An elliptical clause is one from which the subject and all or part of the verb have been dropped as understood, e.g., *while* [I was] *skiing in Banff:*

    Wrong: *While on the wrestling team,* Leo's **dog** came along to practices. [Was the dog on the team?]

Right: *While on the wrestling team,* **Leo** took his dog along to practices.

Right: *While* **Leo** *was* on the wrestling team, his dog came along to practices.

Ellipsis makes sense only when the subject of both clauses is the same, as in the first correct example above (*Leo* is the understood subject of the elliptical clause).

C. Incomplete Comparisons or Expressions of Degree

Wrong: The test was *so easy.*

Right: The test was *so easy that everyone passed.*

Wrong: Prices of some train tickets are higher *than* planes. [illogically compares prices with planes]

Right: Prices of some train tickets are higher *than those of* planes. [compare prices with prices]

D. Needless Shifts

(1) In number:

Wrong: When *a student* fails a test, *they* may grow depressed.

Right: When *a student* fails a test, *she* [or *he*] may grow depressed.

Right: When *students* fail a test, *they* may grow depressed.

This is a matter of agreement; see 24B, page 19. For the *he/she* problem, see 82A(1), page 47.

(2) In person: See 24A, page 19.

(3) In subject or voice of verb:

Wrong: As *I flew* over the city, clogged *roads could be seen.* [*Flew* is active; *could be seen,* passive. Subject shifts from *I* to *roads.*]

Right: As *I flew* over the city, *I could see* clogged roads.

(4) In tense or mood of verb: See 15A, C, pages 9–10.

E. Mixed Construction.
When finishing a sentence, keep in mind how you began it. All its parts should match both grammatically and logically. Remember that the subject must be a noun or something serving as a noun (such as a noun clause or a gerund):

Wrong: *By the Liberals' nominating Wong* makes the NDP's task harder. [The adverb phrase cannot logically be the subject. It tells *how,* not *what.*]

Right: The Liberals' *nomination* of Wong has made the NDP's task harder. [the noun *nomination* made subject]

Wrong: She asked *when did they leave.* [direct-question word order in indirect-question form]

Right: She asked *when they left.* [indirect question]

Right: She asked, *"When did they leave?"* [direct question]

See also, in 80B, pages 44–45, the entry for *reason was because.* For more on indirect questions, see 33A, page 27.

The verb *be* is like an equal sign (=) in mathematics—what is on one side of *be* must be the same, grammatically and logically, as what is on the other:

Wrong: Her favourite *pastime* was *at the movies.* [Pastime does not = place; a pastime is not a place.]

Right: Her favourite *pastime* was *going to the movies.* [pastime = pastime]

Wrong: *Angioplasty* is *when* [or is *where*] a tiny balloon is inserted into an artery. [*When* and *where* refer to time and place, but angioplasty is a procedure, not a time or place.]

Right: *Angioplasty* [procedure] is the *insertion* [procedure] of a tiny balloon into an artery. [procedure = procedure]

Wrong: *Because the National League has more teams* [adverb clause] does not mean *that it has more talent* [noun clause].

Right: *That the National League has more teams* [noun clause] does not mean *that it has more talent* [noun clause].

Right: *Though the National League has more teams* [adverb clause], it does not have more talent [independent clause].

SECTIONS 30–56 Punctuation

Punctuation marks are the traffic signals of writing. They assist the reader through the heavy traffic of ideas that a written passage may contain. Some punctuation marks *separate* words or ideas; others *emphasize* them; still others *group* and *keep together* related ideas. In all, punctuation marks clarify written material that would otherwise confuse and perhaps mislead.

30–32. The Comma [,]

Misuse of the comma accounts for about half of all punctuation errors. The following guidelines, combined with your attention to oral pauses and stops (though commas in writing do not always match oral pauses), should help you solve most comma problems.

30. Use a Comma to Set Off

A. Independent (Main) Clauses. A comma follows the first of two independent clauses that are joined by a coordinating conjunction *(and, but, or, nor, for, yet, so)*:

> The government has spent millions on an AIDS cure, *and* prospects for success are improving.

> Scientists around the world are experimenting with hundreds of drugs, *but* so far the hoped-for cure has proven elusive.

Do *not* use a comma

- Generally, if there is no full clause (subject + verb) after the conjunction:

    > **Wrong:** They voted on the bill Monday, *and* adjourned Tuesday.

    > **Right:** They voted on the bill Monday *and* adjourned Tuesday.

- *After* the conjunction:

    > **Wrong:** They voted on the bill Monday *but,* it was defeated.

    > **Right:** They voted on the bill Monday, *but* it was defeated.

- Between very short independent clauses:

    > **Right:** He lies and she cheats.

- Between independent clauses not joined by a coordinating conjunction (use a semicolon instead):

    > **Wrong:** The starting gun sounded, the crowd roared.

    > **Right:** The starting gun sounded; the crowd roared.

This is a common but serious error. See comma splices and fused sentences, 26B, page 22.

B. Introductory Elements

(1) *An introductory adverb clause:*

> *Whenever war threatens in the Middle East,* world stock markets become jittery.

> *Because the ozone layer was thinning,* skin cancer incidence began to rise.

Note: Usually you do not need a comma when the independent clause comes first: World stock markets become jittery *whenever war threatens in the Middle East.* (But see 30 F(1), page 26, on *because* clauses.)

(2) *A long prepositional phrase or a series of prepositional phrases:*

> *In the aftermath of the scandal,* the director resigned.

Note: Unless clarity demands one, you do not need a comma after one short introductory prepositional phrase: *After the scandal* the director resigned.

(3) *A verbal phrase:*

> *To prevent hostilities,* the UN sent in a peace force.

> *By sending in a force,* the UN prevented hostilities.

> *Encouraged by peace hopes,* stock traders became active.

An infinitive or gerund phrase used as the *subject* of a sentence is not an introductory element. Do not set it off:

> *To prevent hostilities* was the UN's hope.

> *Sending in a peace force* prevented hostilities.

C. Items in a Series. Use commas to separate words, phrases, or clauses in a series of three or more:

> **Words:** A newly released CD contains operatic arias by *Verdi, Puccini, Donizetti,* and *Bellini.*

> **Phrases:** Allied armies pushed *through the French countryside, across the Rhine,* and *into Germany.*

> **Clauses:** *Zelda began ballet lessons, Scott wrote fitfully,* and *together they partied regularly.*

Note: Some writers omit the comma before the final *and* or *or* in a series. Including this comma, however, ensures clarity.
Use a comma before *etc.* at the end of a series: pork, beans, etc.

Do *not* use a comma

- With only two items: She sought *peace* and *quiet.*
- If you repeat *and* or *or* between each two items: She sought *peace* and *quiet* and *solitude.*
- Before the first item or after the last:

    > **Wrong:** She sought, *peace, quiet,* and *solitude.*

    > **Right:** She sought *peace, quiet,* and *solitude.*

    > **Wrong:** *Peace, quiet,* and *solitude,* proved elusive.

    > **Right:** *Peace, quiet,* and *solitude* proved elusive.

D. Coordinate Adjectives. In a series of two or more, use commas to separate adjectives of equal importance. Do not put a comma after the last adjective:

> *Tall, stately* trees lined the roadway.

> Too much *salty, fatty,* or *sugary* food may harm one's health.

Note: Certain combinations of adjectives flow naturally together and need no commas: *little red* schoolhouse; *two creaky old* cars; *additional monetary* demands. Determining when to omit commas is tricky, but if the adjectives would sound odd in a different order (*red little* schoolhouse, *old creaky two* cars, *monetary additional* demands), you probably should omit commas.

E. Parenthetical Expressions. These are words or word groups that interrupt the main flow of thought in a sentence but are not necessary to the sentence; they could be removed from the sentence without changing its essential meaning. Think of the pair of commas almost as parentheses:

They were, *in my opinion*, not guilty.

The jury, *on the other hand*, convicted them all.

The judge, *moreover*, smiled at the verdict.

It is unfortunate, *to be sure*. [Note the great difference in meaning from *It is unfortunate to be sure.*]

Other common parenthetical expressions include *as a matter of fact, to tell the truth, of course, incidentally, namely, in the first place, therefore, thus, consequently, however, nevertheless.*

Note: Not all these expressions are always set off. You may choose not to set off *perhaps, likewise, at least, indeed, therefore, thus,* and certain others in sentences where you feel they do not interrupt your thought flow:

It was, *perhaps*, just an oversight.
It was *perhaps* just an oversight.

F. Non-restrictive (Non-essential) Elements

(1) *Non-restrictive clauses.* A **non-restrictive** clause (usually beginning with *which* or a form of *who*) is parenthetical. The information it gives is *not* essential to the meaning of the sentence. Thus the clause is set off within commas, like other parenthetical elements:

Crestwood Mall, *which Mr. Pappas owns*, is expanding.

Professor Mikasa, *who was born in Japan*, teaches Asian literature.

Read the above sentences, omitting the italicized clauses. Do we still know *which* mall is expanding and *which* professor teaches Asian literature? Yes. The clauses are thus merely parenthetical, not essential; they need commas.

A **restrictive** clause *is* essential to the meaning of the sentence. It fully or partly identifies the preceding noun; it answers the question "which one?" Such a clause is written without commas:

The mall *that Mr. Pappas owns* is expanding.

A professor *who was born in Japan* teaches Asian literature.

Read the above sentences, omitting the italicized clauses. Do we still know *which* mall and *which* professor? No. Without these restrictive clauses the sentences may refer to any mall or any professor. The clauses are therefore essential (restrictive) and take no commas.

One easy way to tell whether a clause is restrictive is to use the *that*-test. Adjective clauses beginning with *that* are always restrictive; so are clauses beginning with *who* or *which* that can be changed to *that* and still sound right:

Restrictive: A professor *who* [or *that*] *was born in Japan* teaches Asian literature. [*That* sounds right.]

Non-restrictive: Professor Mikasa, *who* [but not *that*] *was born in* Japan, teaches Asian literature. [*That* would sound wrong.]

Note: In Canadian usage, *that* is generally preferred over *which* to begin a restrictive clause: The team *that* (rather than *which*) finishes fifth will miss the playoffs.

Note: A *because* clause containing your main point is restrictive:

Peterson lost the 1991 election because he was overconfident. [You assume your reader already knows that Peterson lost; you are stressing the reason he lost.]

A *because* clause giving merely incidental information is non-restrictive:

Classes are being cancelled today, because a water main has broken. [The cancelling is the main point—your reader did not previously know this; the cause is merely incidental.]

(2) *Non-restrictive (non-essential) phrases.* Follow the principle for non-restrictive clauses (see (1) above):

Non-restrictive: The premier, *waving the provincial flag*, led the parade.

Restrictive: A woman *waving the provincial flag* led the parade.

Non-restrictive: Significantly more progress was made by the control group, *composed of five-year-olds.*

Restrictive: Significantly more progress was made by the group *composed of five-year-olds.*

(3) *Non-restrictive appositives:*

The male lead of *Titanic*, *Leonardo DiCaprio*, became an instant teenage idol.

Cobb wrote to his daughter, *Ella*. [The comma shows that the appositive, Ella, is not identifying *which* daughter; thus Cobb must have only one daughter.]

Restrictive appositives take no commas:

The actor *Leonardo DiCaprio* became an instant teenage idol.

Cobb wrote to his daughter *Ella*. [one of two or more daughters]

G. Absolute Phrases (see 21B(2), page 16, for definition)

The ATM having kept his card, Finch had no cash.

Kristi, *her confidence restored*, awaited the interview.

H. Names or Other Words Used in Direct Address

Tell us, *Marlene*, what solution you propose.

Prime Minister, may we quote you on that?

I. *Yes* and *No* at the Beginning of a Sentence

Yes, these lines imply the poet's fear of death.

J. Mild Interjections (expressions of less than strong emotion):

> *Well,* I think it could use more sauce.
>
> *Oh,* just put it down anywhere.

Note: Strong interjections take exclamation points: *Hey!* Come back with my purse.

K. Direct Quotations. Generally, use a comma to set off a direct quotation (someone's exact words) from words that precede, follow, or interrupt it.

> "You can't always get what you want," says the song.
>
> "This," said Miss Marple, "is the final clue."

Punctuation of quotations is treated fully in 44–48, pages 31–32.

L. Examples Introduced by *Such as, Especially, Particularly*; Expressions of Contrast

> She excelled in many sports, *particularly* track.
>
> On weekends we offer several courses, *such as* Biology 101 and Music 210, for non-traditional students.
>
> The class meets in Room 302, *not* 202.

Note: Some *such as* phrases are restrictive: Days *such as* this are rare.

31. Use a Comma Also

A. In Place of Omitted or Understood Words in structures such as

> Hanoi was the northern capital; *Saigon,* the southern. [or, less formally, *Hanoi was the northern capital, Saigon the southern.*]

B. Before a Confirmatory (Tag) Question

> The campus is safe after dark, *isn't it?*

C. In Letters

(1) *After the greeting of a friendly letter:*

> Dear Frank,

Note: Use a colon in a business letter: Dear Mr. Coe:

(2) *After the complimentary close in all letters:*

> Very truly yours,

D. In Dates and Addresses. In a month-day-year date, place the year within commas, as if it were parenthetical. Do the same with the province or country in an address:

> In Lethbridge, *Alberta,* on June 4, *2001,* they were married.

Note: Do not use a comma in a month-year or a day-month-year date or between a province and a postal code: May 1967; 6 June 1944; Victoria, BC V9C 4A1.

E. For Clarity, to Prevent Misreading

> By leaving Nora Helmer gained freedom. [Who left?]
>
> By leaving, Nora Helmer gained freedom. [Nora left.]
>
> By leaving Nora, Helmer gained freedom. [Mr. Helmer left.]

32. Do *Not* Use a Comma

A. To Separate Subject and Verb or Verb and Complement

> ***Wrong:*** Many reference *books, are* now on CD-ROM.
>
> ***Right:*** Many reference *books are* now on CD-ROM.
>
> ***Wrong:*** Savings bonds *provide,* little *income.*
>
> ***Right:*** Savings bonds *provide* little *income.*

B. To Join Two Independent Clauses in Place of a Coordinating Conjunction (*and, but, or, nor, for, yet, so*) or **Semicolon.** Avoiding this serious error, called a *comma splice,* is explained in 26B, page 22.

33–34. The Period [.]

33. Use a Period

A. After Every Sentence Except a Direct Question or an Exclamation

> The *VIA* train goes to Winnipeg. [declarative sentence]
>
> Take the *VIA* train. [imperative sentence]
>
> I'll ask where the *VIA* train goes. [indirect question (a statement about a question); the direct question is "Where does the *VIA* train go?"]

B. After an Abbreviation or Initial

> Mr., Mrs., U.S., Dr., P.E.I., Q.C., M.D., Rev., a.m.

Note: You may write *Ms.* either with or without a period, as long as you are consistent. *Miss* never takes a period.

Do *not* use a period with

- Many well-known sets of initials: IBM, RCMP, CTV, NASA, UN, YWCA, CD-ROM
- Postal abbreviations of provinces: ON, BC, AL
- Radio and television stations: CFAX
- Money in even-dollar denominations: $40
- Contractions: ass'n, sec'y [for *association, secretary.* They may also be written *assn., secy.*]
- Ordinal numbers: 5th, 2nd, Henry VIII
- Nicknames: Rob, Pat, Sid, Pam

- Common shortened terms: memo, math, exam, lab, gym, TV [All these terms are colloquial; use the full words in formal writing.]

C. After a Number or Letter in a Formal Outline

1. Influential Rock Groups

    A. The Tragically Hip

    B. The Bare Naked Ladies

Note: Do *not* use a period

- If the number or letter is within parentheses: (1), (a)
- If the number is part of a title: Chapter 4

D. In a Spaced Group of Three (. . .) to Show

(1) *Ellipsis* (the intentional omission of words) in a quoted passage. Retain necessary punctuation preceding the ellipsis:

- **Customary way:**

    George V. Higgins has written, "I think the only way to find out whether the story in your mind is any good is to sit down by yourself and try to put all of it on paper. . . . If the story interests you enough, . . . it will interest other people."

    The first of the four periods after *paper* signals the end of the sentence. Follow this practice whether the omission is before or after such a period.

- **Latest Modern Language Association way:** Bracket the three periods of any ellipses in quotations to clarify that the ellipses were not in the original. See example, 44F, pages 31–32.

(2) *Pause, hesitation, and the like* in a dialogue and interrupted narrative (do not overuse this device):

> This room. Yes, this room. . . . You . . . was it you? . . . were going out to look for something. . . . The tree of knowledge, wasn't it?
>
> —J. M. Barrie

E. After a Non-sentence. A **non-sentence** is a legitimate unit of expression lacking subject + predicate. It is found mostly in dialogue.

(1) *A greeting:* Good evening.

(2) *A mild exclamation* not within a sentence:

    Oh. Darn.

(3) *An answer to a question:*

    Will you accept? *Perhaps.*

Note: A non-sentence is a correct expression. A fragment (a similar structure *un*intentionally lacking subject + predicate) is an error. Fragments are explained in 26A, pages 21–22.

---

34. Do *Not* Use a Period after a title of a composition or report, even if that title is a sentence:

The Prospects for Health Care Reform

Health Care Can Be Reformed

Do, however, use a question mark or exclamation point where appropriate in a title: *Can Medicare Reform Succeed?*

35–36. The Question Mark [?]

35. Use a Question Mark

A. After a Direct Question

> Did you get a call**?** When**?** From Whom**?**
>
> It was from Mr. Ward, wasn't it**?**
>
> You testified earlier—do you recall**?**—that you didn't know him.
>
> You met him at a party**?** [A question may be in declarative-sentence form; the question mark signals the tone in which it would be spoken.]

For use of the question mark in quotations, see 47C, page 32; in titles, see 34, page 28.

B. Within Parentheses to Indicate Doubt or Uncertainty

> Joan of Arc was born in 1412 (?) and died in 1431.

36. Do *Not* Use a Question Mark

A. After an Indirect Question (see 33A, page 27, for definition)

> Miller asked what the program would cost.

B. After a Polite Request in Question Form

> Would you please sign the enclosed papers.

C. Within Parentheses to Express Humour or Irony

> ***Wrong:*** That purple suit shows his exquisite (?) taste.

37–38. The Exclamation Point [!]

37. Use an Exclamation Point after an emphatic word, sentence, or other expression:

Never!   He has a gun!

How gross!   What a night!

For use of the exclamation point in titles, see 34, page 28. For its use in quotations, see 47C, page 32.

38. Do Not Use an Exclamation Point

A. After a Mild Interjection or a Sentence That Suggests Only Mild Excitement or Emotion. The exclamation point is a strong signal, but one that quickly loses its effect if overused. Except in quoted dialogue, reserve the exclamation point mostly for expressions that begin with *what* or *how* (and are not questions). Elsewhere, use the less dramatic comma or period:

> What a fool I was**!**   Why, I never knew that.

B. More than Once, or with Other Pause or Stop Marks

> *Wrong:* That's a lie!!! [One *!* is sufficient.]
>
> *Wrong:* You failed again?! [Use either *?* or *!*.]

39. The Semicolon [;]

The semicolon signals a greater break in thought than the comma but a lesser break than the period. It is, however, closer to a period than to a comma in most of its uses and is often interchangeable with the period. The semicolon often gives your writing a formal tone, as the following examples suggest.

Use a Semicolon

A. Between Independent Clauses Not Joined by a Coordinating Conjunction

> Commercial architects of the 1950s and 1960s designed huge, unadorned glass boxes**;** Place Ville Marie in Montreal is a landmark of this style.

The semicolon is particularly effective for showing balance or contrast between two clauses:

> The woods abound with wildlife**;** the lakes teem with fish.
>
> First-year students think they know nothing**;** second-year students know they know everything.

B. Between Independent Clauses Joined by a Conjunctive Adverb *(therefore, however, nevertheless, thus, moreover, also, besides, consequently, meanwhile, otherwise, then, furthermore, likewise, in fact, still)*:

> Years ago many Canadian university diplomas were written in Latin**;** *however,* today very few are.
>
> For early feminists, voting rights were the key to equality**;** *consequently,* these women focussed on suffrage.

Note: The comma after some conjunctive adverbs is optional.

Even when the conjunctive adverb moves into the second clause, the semicolon stays put between the clauses:

> Years ago many Canadian university diplomas were written in Latin**;** today, *however,* very few are.

C. Between Independent Clauses Joined by a Coordinating Conjunction When There Are Commas Within the Clauses

> Today we take for granted automobile safety equipment such as air bags, collapsible steering columns, and antilock brakes**;** *yet* fifty years ago cars were not required even to have directional signals, seat belts, or outside rear-view mirrors. [The semicolon marks the break between the independent clauses more clearly than another comma would.]

D. Between Items in a Series When There Are Commas Within the Items

> The new officers are Verna Brooks, chair**;** Henri LeClerc, social director**;** Sam Lee, treasurer**;** and Sharon Grady, secretary.

40–42. The Apostrophe [']

40. Use an Apostrophe with Possessive Nouns.

Possessive nouns show "belonging to." If your cousin has (possesses) a car, the car belongs to your cousin. It is your cousin**'s** car, the car of your cousin. Possessive nouns always add an apostrophe ('). Singular possessive nouns normally also add an *s* (**'s**).

You can identify a possessive noun by trying it at the end of an *of* phrase; if it makes sense there, it is possessive: the beak *of a bird* → *a bird's* beak; the nose of Arthur → *Arthur's* nose; the team *of the girls* → the *girls'* team.

A. Use Apostrophe + s ('s) with—	B. Use Apostrophe Alone (')with—
• Almost all singular nouns: a woman**'s** coat Ms. Bonilla**'s** cats Mr. Bates**'s** house an eagle**'s** nest a person**'s** legal right a fox**'s** bushy tail the class**'s** record	• Plural nouns ending in *s*: the two girls**'** coats the Bonillas**'** cats the Bateses**'** house all the eagles**'** nests the boys**'** gymnasium the foxes**'** bushy tails the classes**'** records
• Plural nouns that do not end in *s*: women**'s** rights the people**'s** voice the geese**'s** flight	• A few singular names that would sound awkward with another *s*: Ulysses**'** travels Sophocles**'** irony

Note: Some editors favour adding only an apostrophe to singular nouns ending in *s*: *Ms. Bates', class'*. Whichever system you follow be consistent.

Caution: Do not confuse the ordinary plural of nouns with the possessive. Ordinary plural: I know the Bonillas. Possessive plural: The Bonillas' cat died. See 42B, page 30.

C. Use Possessives Before Gerunds (Verbal Nouns). Just as you would say *Kirsch's action shocked everyone,* say **Kirsch's quitting** shocked everyone and *We were shocked by* **Kirsch's quitting** *without notice.* Other examples: *The UN protested the* **terrorists' bombing** *of the town. Horace disliked the* **store's closing** *early on weekends.*

D. Note These Fine Points of Possession:

(1) *Joint vs. individual possession:* If two or more nouns possess something jointly, only the last noun gets an apostrophe:

> *Jennifer and Rod's* new baby is a girl.

If each noun possesses a separate thing, each noun gets its own apostrophe:

> *Jennifer's* and *Maria's* babies are both girls.

(2) *Hyphenated words:* Add the apostrophe to the last word only:

> Her *brother-in-law's* job was eliminated.

(3) *Possessive pronouns* can be confusing. Possessive indefinite and reciprocal pronouns take an apostrophe, just like nouns: *anybody's, someone's, each other's, one another's, someone else's, everybody else's,* . . . (see 18D, page 13, for full list). But possessive personal pronouns never take an apostrophe: *yours, his, hers, its, ours, theirs;* nor does *whose. Its* and *whose,* particularly, cause problems because they look much like the contractions for *it is* and *who is* (see 41A and 42A below; 19F(3), page 15; and 83, pages 48–52.)

(4) *Words expressing time or amount* usually form their possessives just as other nouns do: *a dollar's worth, a moment's rest, a week's pay, two weeks' pay.*

41. Use an Apostrophe Also

A. To Show Contractions and Other Omissions of Letters or Numerals

can't [cannot]	what's [what is]	it's [it is]
who's [who is]	we're [we are]	they're [they are]
you're [you are]	storm of '99 [1999]	fishin' [fishing]

B. To Form the Plurals of Letters and Symbols

> Her grades included three *A*'**s** and two *B*'**s.**
>
> Use +'**s** and -'**s** on the test.

Use the apostrophe only where clarity demands it. You generally do not need it with figures (the 1990s, hitting in the .300s), words referred to as words (*if*s, *and*s or *but*s), or initials (*YWCA*s).

42. Do Not Use an Apostrophe

A. With Possessive Personal Pronouns (*his, hers, its, ours, yours, theirs*) or with *whose*

> *Whose* sales team has surpassed *its* quota? Is it *hers, yours,* or *theirs?* It could be *ours.* [See 19F(3), page 15, and 83, pages 48–52, for *its/it's,* etc.]

B. With Ordinary Plurals or Verbs

> The *Browns* went to the *stores.* Countless *stars* appeared. [ordinary plurals, not possessive]
>
> The mayor *says* no, but she *means* perhaps. [verbs ending in s]

C. To Form the Possessives of Inanimate Objects (generally—unless an *of* phrase sounds awkward):

> ***Poor:*** her *shoe's* sole
>
> ***Better:*** the sole *of her* shoe

But

> ***Awkward:*** the pay *of a week*
>
> ***Better:*** a *week's* pay

43. Italics (Underlining)

Italic type, or *italics,* is slanted type, like the first words of this sentence. Generally, in your word processing, typing, or handwriting, indicate italics by underlining: <u>The Diviners</u>, <u>The Diviners</u>. However, if using Columbia Online Style (see 95A(3) and 95C, pages 60–61), use actual italics. Also see note, 95C, page 61.

Note: Some publications, especially some magazines and newspapers, follow styles that omit all or most italics. Though not wrong, such alternative styles are not recommended.

Use Italics to Designate

A. Titles of Separate Publications

(1) *Books:* Our readings include Richler's *Barney's Version.*

(2) *Magazines, newspapers, and journals:* Her subscriptions range from the *Georgia Straight* to *Popular Mechanics.*

> *Note:* The word *the* is not capitalized or italicized in a newspaper or magazine title.

(3) *Bulletins, pamphlets, and newsletters:* CRD
Conservation Tips.

(4) *Plays, films, TV and radio programs, and musical productions:*

> *Napoleon* [play or musical production]
>
> *The Sweet Hereafter* [film]
>
> *The Newsroom* [TV or radio program. For a single segment or episode in a series, use quotation marks: "The Meltdown."]

(5) *Poems long enough to be published alone as books:*

> Homer's *Iliad*

(6) *Electronic publications (tapes, compact discs, computer programs, CD-ROMs, online databases . . .):*

> *Globe and Mail Online*

Note: Do not underline (or put within quotation marks) the title at the beginning of a composition or research paper unless the title contains words that would be underlined anyway, such as the title of a novel:

> Symbolism in Munro's Early Stories
> Symbolism in Munro's *Lives of Girls and Women*

B. Names of Ships, Aircraft, and Spacecraft

> The *Alaska Princess* sails from Vancouver.
>
> The space shuttle *Endeavour* landed on schedule.

C. Titles of Paintings and Sculptures

> *Morning Sun*   Michelangelo's *David*   *The Blue Boy*

D. Foreign Words Not Yet Anglicized

> The lovers bade each other *sayonara.*

Note: Generally, if a word is listed in a reputable English dictionary, it is considered anglicized and needs no italics. Do not underline the common abbreviations a.m., p.m., A.D., viz., vs., etc., i.e., e.g.

E. Words, Letters, Figures, or Symbols Referred to as Such

> Remember the *d* when spelling *supposed to.*
>
> His licence number contained two *J*'s and a *9.*
>
> Avoid using *&* for *and* in formal writing.

F. Emphasis, where you cannot convey it by the order or choice of your words:

> Ms. Coe said that she *might* reconsider the grade. [The emphasis on *might* stresses the uncertainty.]

Note: Avoid overuse of italics for emphasis.

44–48. Quotation Marks [" "]

Quotation marks enclose the exact words of a speaker, certain titles, or words used in a special sense. Quotation marks are always (with one small exception) used in pairs.

44. Use Regular (Double) Quotation Marks [" "] to Enclose a Direct Quotation.

A. Use Quotation Marks Around a Speaker's Exact Words. Note that commas set off each quotation:

> She said, "I'll see you in court."
>
> "I'll see you in court," she said.
>
> She said, "I'll see you in court," and left.

Note: Do not use quotation marks with an *indirect* quotation (a paraphrase or summary of a speaker's words): She told him that she would see him in court.

B. With an Interrupted Quotation, use quotation marks around only the quoted words:

> "I'll see you," she said, "in court."

C. With an *Uninterrupted* Quotation of More than One Sentence, use quotation marks only before the first sentence and after the last:

> *Wrong:* She said, "You can't deny me my rights."
> "I'll see you in court."
>
> *Right:* She said, "You can't deny me my rights. I'll see you in court."

D. With an *Uninterrupted* Quotation of Several Paragraphs, use either of the following forms:

- Put quotation marks at the beginning of *each* paragraph but at the end of only the *last* paragraph.
- Use no quotation marks at all; instead, type the entire quotation as an indented block. See 60C, page 36.

E. With a Short Quotation That Is Only Part of a Sentence, use no commas:

> They had promised to "show some muscle."

F. Use Three Spaced Periods to Show Omission of unimportant or irrelevant words from a quotation (ellipsis—see 33D(1), page 28).

- **Customary way:**

> Emerson wrote, "Is it so bad, then to be misunderstood? . . . To be great is to be misunderstood."

- **Latest Modern Language Association style,** using brackets to show that the ellipsis was not in the original (keep all the original punctuation in its proper place outside the brackets):

> Emerson wrote, **"**Is it so bad, then, to be misunderstood? [**. . .**] To be great is to be misunderstood.**"**

G. To Insert Your Explanatory Words Into a Quotation, use brackets (not parentheses). See 54A, page 34.

H. When Quoting Dialogue, start a new paragraph with each change of speaker:

> **"**The lead guitarist is superb,**"** she remarked.
>
> **"**He sounds tinny to me,**"** I replied.

I. When Quoting Poetry, use quotation marks only for very short passages (three lines or less) that are run into your text. Use a slash mark (with a space before and after) to show the end of each line of the poem:

> Leonard Cohen writes that **"**the sun pours down like honey **/** On Our Lady of the Harbour.**"**

For quotations of more than three lines, do not use quotation marks; type the lines as an indented block as explained in 60C (page 34).

45. Use Double Quotation Marks Also to Enclose

A. Titles of Short Written Works: Poems, Articles, Essays, Short Stories, Chapters, Songs

> **"**Hemingway Set His Own Hours**"** is an essay in *Broadsides.*
>
> Chapter 3 of *The Trolls* is titled **"**Green.**"**
>
> **"**Daddy's Little Girl**"** is a favourite wedding song.

B. Definition of Words

> The word *nice* once meant **"**foolish or wanton.**"**

C. Words Used in a Special Sense or for a Special Purpose

> [A]nti-drug agents detained two brothers accused of being [. . .] producers of methamphetamines, or **"**speed.**"**
>
> —*National Post*

If you are using the word several times within a short paper or chapter, you need quotation marks only the first time.

Note: Occasionally you will see a slang expression or nickname enclosed in quotation marks, indicating that the writer recognizes the expression to be inappropriately informal. Avoid this apologetic use of quotation marks.

46. Use Single Quotation Marks [' '] to enclose a

quotation within a quotation. Think of this construction as a box within a box. Ordinary double quotation marks [" "] provide the wrapping around the outer box; single quotation marks [' '] provide the wrapping around the inner box. Be sure to place end punctuation within the correct box:

> "Who said, 'Alas! poor Yorick' ?" the dean asked.

47. Use Other Marks with Quotation Marks as Follows:

A. Periods and Commas. Always put these marks inside closing quotation marks:

> **"**Stocks are up,**"** he said. **"**Bonds may fall.**"**

B. Colons and Semicolons. Always put these marks *outside* closing quotation marks:

> He announced, **"**Stocks are up**"**; then they fell.
>
> There have been two popular recordings of **"**Farewell to Nova Scotia**"**: Ian and Sylvia's and Stompin' Tom's.

C. Question Marks, Exclamation Points, and Dashes. Place these marks *inside* the quotation marks when they belong to the quotation, *outside* otherwise:

> Luz asked, **"**Which key do I press**?"** [The quotation is the question.]
>
> Did Luz say, **"**I clicked the mouse**"?** [The part outside the quotation is the question.]
>
> Did Luz ask, **"**Which key do I press**"?** [Both the quotation and the outside part are questions. Use only one question mark—the outside one.]
>
> **"**It's perfect**!"** Luz exclaimed.
>
> How wonderful it was when Luz said, **"**Now I understand**"!**
>
> **"**I don't see how—**"** Luz began, but she kept trying.
>
> **"**Now**"**—Luz grabbed the printout—**"**let's see it.**"**

48. Do Not Use Quotation Marks

A. To Enclose the Title Introducing a Composition or Research Paper (unless the title is a quotation):

> *Wrong:* "The Federal Election of 2000"
>
> *Right:* The Federal Election of 2000

B. To Show Intended Irony, Humour, or Emphasis. Your irony or humour will be more effective if not so blatantly pointed out:

> *Wrong:* His "golden" voice emptied the opera house.
>
> *Right:* His golden voice emptied the opera house.

For emphasis, use italics (see 43F, page 31).

49–50. The Colon [:]

49. Use a Colon to Introduce

A. A List That Follows a Grammatically Complete Statement. The list is usually in apposition to some word in the statement:

> Their journey took them to four countries: Turkey, Iran, Pakistan, and India. [The four names are in apposition to *countries*.]

> Only one traveller was a native Asian: Ibrahim. [*Ibrahim* is a one-item "list" in apposition to *traveller*.]

Often *the following* or *as follows* precedes the colon:

> Their papers included *the following*: passports, visas, health records, and driver's licences.

Do *not* use a colon after an *in*complete statement (one that lacks, for example, a needed complement or object of preposition), or after *such as* or *for example:*

> **Wrong:** Their papers included: passports, visas, health records, and driver's licences.

> **Right:** Their papers included passports, visas. . . .

> **Wrong:** Their journey took them to countries *such as:* Turkey, Iran, Pakistan, and India.

> **Right:** Their journey took them to countries *such as* Turkey, Iran. . . .

B. A Long Quotation (one or more paragraphs):

> In *The Swinging Flesh* Irving Layton wrote: Like all artists, I am concerned with Appearance and Reality and with the traffic that goes on between them. [Quotation continues for one or more paragraphs.]

C. A Formal Quotation or Question

> Cutting the tape, the mayor declared: "The Hillman Trail is officially open."

> The basic question is: where [or *Where*] is our country headed?

D. A Second Independent Clause That Explains or Illustrates the First Clause

> There is a way to win the election: we [or *We*] can play up the incumbent's shady past.

E. The Body of a Business Letter (after the greeting):

> Dear Madam: Dear Dr. Schwartz:

Note: Use a comma after the greeting of a personal (friendly) letter.

F. The Details Following an Announcement

> For rent: room with kitchen, near campus.

G. A Formal Resolution, After the Word *Resolved*

> Resolved: That the club spend $50 for decorations.

H. The Words of a Speaker in a Play (after the speaker's name):

> ROSALIND: Nay, but who is it?

50. Use a Colon to Separate

A. Parts of a Title, Reference, or Numeral

> *Title:* The Cold War: A Reinterpretation

> *Reference:* Isaiah 10:3–15 [or, in MLA style, 10.3–15]

> *Numeral:* 11:25 p.m.

B. Certain Parts of a Bibliography Entry

> Palango, Paul. <u>The Last Guardians: The Crisis in the RCMP</u>. Toronto: McClelland & Stewart, 1998.

> Colón, Rafael Hernández. "Doing Right by Puerto Rico." *Foreign Affairs* 77.4 (1998): 112–114.

See 95C, page 61, for details of bibliographic styles.

51. The Dash [—]

The dash is a dramatic mark, signalling an abrupt break in the flow of a sentence. Do not use it for an ordinary pause or stop, in place of a comma, period, or semicolon. When typing, make a dash by using two strokes of the hyphen key, with no spaces before, between, or after--like this.

Use a Dash

A. To Show a Sudden Break in Thought

> I'm sure it was last Novem—no, it was October.

> If you don't apologize at once, I'll—

> "My dear constituents, I greet you—" the MP began, but he was stopped by a chorus of boos.

B. To Set Off a Parenthetical Element that is long, that sharply interrupts the sentence, or that otherwise would be hard to distinguish:

> World War I—my grandfather called it "the big war"—was shorter than World War II.

> Thus, it was disconcerting to see Alberta's reformers accelerate the exposure of the province's consumers—of all sizes—to the market.
>
> —*Globe and Mail*

C. To Emphasize an Appositive

He had only one goal—stardom. [or . . . *goal: stardom.*]

Sarah, Vera, Maria, Tammy—all have found better jobs.

Three majors—literature, writing, and linguistics—are offered in this department.

Note: The colon can also emphasize an appositive, but it imparts a more formal tone than the dash.

D. To Precede the Author's Name After a Direct Quotation

The lack of power corrupts. The absolute lack of power corrupts absolutely.

—Pierre Trudeau

52–53. Parentheses [( )]

52. Use Parentheses (Always in Pairs)

A. To Set Off Incidental Information or Comments

Keith Martin **(**MP for Juan de Fuca**)** spoke against the bill.

The old washing machine **(**it predates Woodstock and probably the Beatles**)** still does three loads a day.

Note: Do not overuse parentheses. Use commas to set off ordinary parenthetical (interrupting) expressions. Do not use an opening capital letter or closing period with a sentence in parentheses within a larger sentence.

B. To Enclose

(1) *Letters or figures in enumeration:*

The secretary must **(**1**)** take minutes at meetings, **(**2**)** do all typing, and **(**3**)** keep records.

(But see 33C, page 28.)

(2) *References and directions:*

The amoeba **(**see figure 6**)** reproduces asexually.

(3) *A question mark indicating uncertainty:*

She was born in China in 1778(?) and died in 1853.

C. For Accuracy, in Legal Documents and Business Letters

Please remit the sum of fifty dollars **(**$50**)**.

D. With Other Punctuation Marks as Follows:

(1) *The comma, semicolon, and period* follow the closing parenthesis in a sentence:

Her longest novel **(**687 pages**)**, it is also her best.

She speaks Greek **(**her family's tongue**)**; he speaks Russian.

The heat grew unbearable **(**it broke the record**)**.

(2) *The question mark and the exclamation point* go inside the parentheses if the mark belongs to the parenthetical element; otherwise, they go outside:

The book mentions Mechthild of Magdeburg **(**died 1282**?).**

Have you read much of Samuel Butler **(**died 1680**)?**

Sid asked me to lend him $50 **(**what nerve**!).**

53. Do Not Use Parentheses

A. To Indicate Deletions. Instead draw a line through the deleted words:

Wrong: Gary Doer was elected in 1995 **(**and 1999**)**.

Right: Gary Doer was elected in 1995 ~~and 1999~~.

B. To Enclose Your Editorial Comment. Use brackets for this purpose, as explained in the next section.

54. Brackets [[ ]]

Use Brackets

A. To Enclose Your Editorial or Explanatory Remarks Within a Direct Quotation

According to Antonia Fraser, "As Queen, however, she **[**Katherine Howard**]** had new ways of enjoying herself: the exercise of patronage, for example."

See 44F, pages 31–32, for use of brackets with ellipses in quotations.

B. With *sic* to Mark the Original Writer's Error in Material You Are Quoting

His letter said, "I'm not use **[**sic**]** to rejection."

Sic is Latin for "Thus it is." Its use clarifies that the error was made not by you but by the person you are quoting.

C. To Enclose Stage Directions

JUAN **[***striding to the door***]**: Someone must help them.

55. The Hyphen [-]

Use a Hyphen

A. To Join Certain Compound Words

sister-in-law   will-o'-the-wisp   Scottish-Irish

A good dictionary will show which compounds are hyphenated. Generally, if the compound is not in the dictionary, write it as two words, with no hyphen: *tree trunk*.

B. To Join Words Used as a Single Adjective Before a Noun

a well-known author late-model cars fifty-dollar bill

a now-you-see-me-now-you-don't office presence

cat-and-mouse game

Note: Do not hyphenate such a modifier when it *follows* a noun as a subjective complement: Hanley is *well known*. Do not use a hyphen between an *-ly* adverb and an adjective: *freshly baked* bread. With a series of hyphenated modifiers, omit the part after the hyphen until the last item: *ten-, twenty-, and fifty-dollar bills*.

C. When Writing Out Two-Word Numbers from Twenty-One to Ninety-Nine and Two-Word Fractions

thirty-three sixty-seven

ninety-eighth four-fifths

But other words in the number take no hyphen:

four hundred and fifteen four hundred and twenty-five

five twenty-fourths one thousand four hundred and twenty-five

Also hyphenate a compound adjective containing a number:

ten-year-old boy forty-hour week

hundred-yard dash ten-dollar bill

two- and three-room apartments

See sections 65, 66 and 67, pages 39–40, for guidelines on using figures versus writing out numbers.

D. To Avoid Ambiguity

Ambiguous: Mitchell was the *senior housing director*. [*senior director of housing* or *director of housing for seniors*?]

Clear: Mitchell was the *senior-housing director*. [director of housing for seniors. For the other meaning, use *senior director of housing*.]

E. With the Prefixes *ex-* (When It Means "Former"), *self-*, and *all-*, and the Suffix *-elect*

ex-manager self-pity

all-county Mayor-elect Bobbs

Note: Today many prefixes and suffixes are joined to root words without hyphens, except where ambiguity *(recover, re-cover)* or awkwardness might result or where the root is capitalized *(anti-American, Europe-wide)*. Examples of current usage are *antioxidant* (but *anti-personnel*), *nonconformist* (but *non-custodial*), *semifinal* (but *semi-conscious*), *bimonthly, nationwide* (but *city-wide*). Consult a good dictionary for current usage.

F. To Indicate Words That Are Spelled Out and Hesitation or Stammering

"It's her time for b-e-d," the child's mother said.

"It's c-c-cold in h-here," he stammered.

G. To Divide a Word That Will Not Fit at the End of a Line. For example, see line 3 of 60A, next page.

Note: Always put the hyphen at the end of the first line, not at the beginning of the second line. Do not guess where a word should divide; consult your dictionary. See 64, page 39, for more details on syllabication.

56. The Slash (Virgule) [/]

Use a Slash

A. Between Two Lines of Poetry Quoted in Running Text

Zoe Landale invokes family life as "The structure of meals a ritual which **/** held back chaos." [Leave a space before and after the slash.]

See 44I, page 32.

B. Between Alternatives

This bus stops at Pandora Street**/**Main Street [alternative names for the same street].

The new Dodge**/**Plymouth is on special sale [different brand names for the same car].

For *and/or*, see 81, pages 45–47. Do not use the slash for a hyphen: *Calgary-Edmonton* (not *Calgary/Edmonton*) flights.

C. To Mean *per:* $1.65/kg

D. In Fractions: 5/8 x/2

SECTIONS 60–74 Mechanics and Spelling

The technical conventions that apply only to the written form of our language, such as capitalization and number form, are called mechanics. (Punctuation, too, is part of mechanics but warrants a division of its own in this book.) Attention to spelling and other mechanical details signals that you are a careful writer, concerned about your paper's appearance, readability, and clarity.

60. Manuscript Form

A. Handwritten Papers. Use white, lined paper that is 21.7 x 28 cm (8 1/2 by 11 inches). Write on one side of the paper only, using black or blue ink. Do not use paper torn from notebooks. Write legibly; a word difficult to decipher may be marked as an error. Clearly distinguish between capital and lower-case letters.

B. Papers Composed on Computers or Typed. If working on a computer or typewriter, make sure you have enough ink for your entire project. In both cases, use high quality, unlined, white paper; type or print on one side only. Choose a plain font such as Times New Roman or Courier and a font size of 12 points. Unless otherwise instructed, leave a 2.5 cm (one inch) margin at the top, bottom, and sides of the paper. Turn on pagination if available.

C. Spacing. Whether handwriting, typing, or word processing, use double spacing and leave one-inch margins all around (see 96, page 66). To begin a paragraph, indent five spaces (1/2 inch in handwriting). Do not indent the first line of a page unless it begins a paragraph. Do not crowd lines at the bottom of a page; use a new sheet.

Separate from the text any prose quotations longer than four lines or verse quotations longer than three lines; use no quotation marks, indent 10 spaces from the left margin (2.5 cm or one inch in handwriting), and maintain double spacing. Keep shorter quotations in the body of your text, and enclose them in quotation marks. See 44I, page 32, and 95A, pages 59–60.

D. Titles and Page Numbers. For placing of titles, see 96A, page 66. For punctuation and capitalization of titles, see 34, page 28; 48A, page 32; and 61F, page 37.

Number all pages with Arabic numerals (1, 2 . . .) in the upper right corner, with no periods or parentheses. If using MLA style, precede each page number with your last name; if using APA, instead of your last name use a short form of your title. See 96, page 66, for examples.

E. Justifying and Word Dividing. *Right justifying* means making every line of text end precisely at the right margin. (Most word-processing systems can do this.) However, unless your instructor permits, do *not* right justify your papers. Also,

unless your instructor permits, do not divide a word at the end of a line when the whole word will not fit. Put it on the next line. (Most computers do this automatically or have a command that will cancel hyphenation).

F. Proofreading. Before handing in a paper, examine it several times for errors in typing, spelling, punctuation, wording, and sentence construction. Computer spelling checkers are generally not smart enough to catch homonyms (*there* for *their*) or wrong words correctly spelled (*drams* for *dreams*), and grammar checkers can be wildly imprecise. If you have many errors, redo the page or even the whole paper, especially if you are word processing. If you have only a few minor errors, make changes neatly, as follows:

(1) *Deletions.* Draw a horizontal line through words to be deleted. Do not use parentheses. See 53A, page 34.

(2) *Insertions.* Above the line write the words to be inserted, and just below the line use a caret (∧) to show the point of insertion.

(3) *Paragraphing.* Use the ¶ sign to show the point at which you wish to begin a paragraph. Write *NO ¶* if you wish to remove a paragraph indention.

61–63. Capitalization

61. Capitalize

A. The First Word of Every Sentence, including quoted sentences:

> The network declared, "The war has definitely ended."

But do *not* capitalize the first word of

- An indirect quotation (paraphrase): The network declared *that the war had ended.*
- A fragmentary quotation: The network declared that the war had "definitely ended."
- A sentence in parentheses within another sentence: The network declared (everyone assumed it true) that the war had ended. This rule applies also with dashes; see 51B, page 33.

B. The First Word of a Line of Poetry (unless the poet has used lower case):

> **U**nhappy we the setting sun deplore,
>
> **S**o glorious once, but ah! it shines no more.
>
> —Phyllis Wheatley

C. Words and Phrases Used as Sentences

> **W**hen? **N**ever **N**o, not you. **O**f course.

D. The First Word of a Formal Question or Statement Following a Colon

> The border guard questioned us: **W**hat is your destination? **H**ow long will you stay?
>
> McLuhan said it best: **T**he medium is the message.

E. The First Word of Each Item in a Formal Outline

> 1. **E**xercises to develop shoulder muscles
>   A. **L**ateral raise
>   B. **P**ullover

F. Important Words in a Title

> *Death Comes for the Archbishop* [book]
>
> "**S**ex, **B**etrayal, and **M**urder" [article]

Always capitalize the first and the last word. Capitalize all other words *except*

> **(1) Articles (a, an, and the):**
>
> *Driving off the Map*
>
> **(2) Prepositions (on, of, to . . .) and to in an infinitive:**
>
> *Dictionary of Canadian Biography*   *A Night to Remember*
>
> **(3) Coordinating conjunctions (and, but . . .):**
>
> *Life and Times*

Note: Some authorities favour capitalizing prepositions and conjunctions of four or more letters, such as *about: Much Ado About Nothing.* Most authorities favour not capitalizing *the* beginning a newspaper or magazine title: The story was in *the Montreal Gazette.* Always capitalize the first word following a dash or colon in a title: *Tokyo at Night: A Guide to Restaurants and Clubs.*

G. The First and Last Words in the Salutation (Greeting) of a Letter and the First Word in the Complimentary Close

> **M**y dearest **S**on,   **V**ery truly yours,

H. The Pronoun *I* and the Interjection *O* (but not oh):

> To thee, **O** Lord, **I** pray.   Why, **o**h why?

62. Capitalize Proper Nouns. A proper noun, as distinguished from a common noun, is the name of a

specific person, place, or thing: *Milton, Canada, Eiffel Tower.* (A proper adjective, made from a proper noun, is also capitalized: *Miltonic, Canadian.*)

Proper Noun	Common Noun
Tamara	woman
Vatican **C**ity	city
October	month
Camosun **C**ollege	college
Rockville **F**ire **D**epartment	organization

A. Specific Persons, Ethnic Groups, Tribes, Nationalities, Religions, and Languages

John **R**alston **S**aul	**C**aucasian	**H**ispanic
Iroquois	**Q**uebecois	**I**slam

Note: Most style manuals, though not all, favour lower-casing *black, white, aborigine,* and other racial descriptions. Whichever style you choose, be consistent with all races.

B. Specific Places (countries, states, cities, geographic sections; oceans, lakes, and other bodies of water; streets, buildings, rooms, parks, monuments, and so forth):

Tanzania	**A**rctic **O**cean	**S**outh **M**ain **S**treet
New **B**runswick	the **P**acific **R**im	the **B**arr **B**uilding
Greenville	**R**oom 67	**L**ake **H**uron
Hyde **P**ark	the **C**enotaph	
Lakes **E**rie and **H**uron (but *the Fraser and Red Rivers*)		

C. Specific Organizations, Companies, and Brand Names

The **B**lue **J**ays	**U**nited **N**ations	**B**oard of **H**ealth
United **C**hurch	the **R**ed **C**ross	**T**remblant **S**ki **C**lub
Liberal **P**arty	**S**upreme **C**ourt	**A**ce **T**ire **C**orp.
Juicy **F**ruit gum [lower-case the product]		

D. Days of the Week, Months, Holidays, and Holy Days

Tuesday	**M**arch	**C**anada **D**ay	**M**other's **D**ay
Labour **D**ay	**E**aster	**Y**om **K**ippur	**R**amadan

E. Religious Names Considered Sacred

> **G**od (but *the gods*) the **A**lmighty the **V**irgin **A**llah

Note: The modern tendency is not to capitalize pronouns referring to the Deity except to avoid ambiguity: Trust in *Him.* But *May God shed his grace on you.*

F. Historical Events, Periods, and Documents

the **G**ulf **W**ar	the **B**attle of **W**aterloo
the **G**reat **D**epression	the **R**enaissance
Magna **C**arta	**C**harter of **R**ights

But *20th century, feminist movement, mysticism*

G. Educational Institutions, Departments, Specific Courses, and Specific Academic Degrees

McGill **U**niversity   **B**iology 101 [but see 63D, page 38]

Ph.D.   **D**epartment of **M**usic

H. Flags, Awards, and School Colours

the **M**aple **L**eaf   the **J**uno **A**ward

the **G**iller **P**rize   the **B**lue and **G**old

I. Stars and Planets

the **N**orth **S**tar   **S**aturn   the **B**ig **D**ipper

Note: Do not capitalize *sun* and *moon* unless they are personified (considered as persons). Do not capitalize *earth* unless it is personified or considered as one of the planets.

J. Ships, Trains, Aircraft, and Spacecraft

HMCS *Halifax*   *Silver Meteor*   *Endeavour*

K. Initials and Other Letter Combinations indicating time, divisions of government, letter equivalents of telephone numbers, call letters of radio and TV stations, and certain other well-known letter combinations:

B.C. (or **B.C.E.**)	**TV**	1-800-**SKI HERE**
RCMP	**O.K.** (or **OK**)	**AIDS**
CJAD	**A.D.** (or **C.E.**)	**CBC**

L. Personifications

Mother **N**ature   **O**ld **M**an **W**inter   the hand of **D**eath

M. Titles Preceding Names

Professor Che-Tsao Chang   **C**hief **J**ustice McLachlin

General Mackenzie   the **R**everend Peale

Do not capitalize a title following a name unless the title shows very high national or international distinction:

Che-Tsao Chang, **p**rofessor of art

Elizabeth II, **Q**ueen of Canada

You may capitalize a title of very high distinction when used instead of the person's name. Be consistent in this usage:

The **P**remier greeted the **P**ope.

Capitalize an abbreviated title before or after a name:

Prof. Maura Ryan, **Ph.D.**   **D**r. Homer Page, **Jr.**

63. Do *Not* Capitalize

A. Points of the Compass

The trail led **n**orth by **n**orthwest.

But do capitalize such words when referring to sections of the nation or world (usually preceded by *the*):

Provinces in the **W**est and **M**aritimes are gaining population.

The **M**iddle **E**ast's perspective differs from the **W**est's.

B. Seasons (unless personified):

The South is warm in **w**inter, hot in **s**ummer.

. . . crown old **W**inter's head with flowers.

—Richard Crashaw

C. Words Denoting a Family Relationship, when they follow a possessive noun or pronoun:

She is Jorge's **a**unt.   My **f**ather has just left.

But do capitalize when the family relationship is used as a title preceding a name or by itself as a name:

Jorge greeted **A**unt Julia.   Come back, **F**ather.

D. Names of Academic Disciplines (unless they are part of specific course titles or proper nouns):

The college offers courses in **f**inance and **m**arketing.

The college offers **F**inance 101 and **M**arketing 203. [specific course titles]

Courses in **C**hinese and **J**apanese are also available. [proper nouns]

E. Common Nouns (unless they are part of proper nouns):

The fire **d**epartment from a **r**ural **d**istrict won the fire-fighting **c**ontest at the local **h**igh **s**chool.

The **M**etchosin **F**ire **B**rigade from the **S**ooke **D**istrict won the **A**ll-**B**ritish **C**olumbia **F**irefighters' **C**ontest at **B**elmont **H**igh **S**chool.

F. Common Words Derived from Proper Nouns

french fries   **c**hina [dishes]   **r**oman numerals

G. The First Word After a Semicolon

She wanted to travel; **h**e wanted to stay put.

H. The First Word in the Latter Part of an Interrupted Quotation (unless that word begins a new sentence):

"English 405," Ralph insisted, "**w**ill do wonders for your writing." [All quoted words are one sentence.]

"Take English 405," Ralph insisted. "**I**t will do wonders for your writing." [*It* begins a new quoted sentence.]

I. The First Word of a Quotation That Is Only Part of a Sentence

Her courage was called "**a**bove and beyond duty."

J. The Second Part of Most Compound Words (unless the second part is a proper noun):

Thirty-**f**ifth Avenue   Mayor-**e**lect Hirsch

anti-**A**merican

K. A Word That You Want to Emphasize (use italics instead):

> **Wrong:** You were told NOT to go there.
>
> **Right:** You were told *not* to go there.

64. Syllabication

The need to divide a word that will not fit at the end of a line has been eliminated in most word processing, which can automatically move the whole word to the next line (see 60E, page 36). Nevertheless, knowledge of word-division principles is important for other writing occasions.

Avoid dividing any words if at all possible; especially avoid breaking two successive lines. When breaking a word is unavoidable, mark the division with a hyphen (made with one keyboard stroke [-]). A good dictionary is your most reliable guide to the hyphenation of words. Remembering the following rules, however, will reduce your need to consult the dictionary.

A. Divide According to Pronunciation; Always Divide Between Syllables. Leave enough of a word at the end of the first line to suggest the sound and meaning of the whole word: *con-vince, irreg-ular, change-able.*

B. Divide Compound Words Between the Parts: *hand-book, book-keeper, rattle-snake.* If a compound word is already hyphenated, break it at an existing hyphen: *sister-in-law, self-portrait.*

C. Do Not Divide a One-Syllable Word of any Length: *thoughts, straight, clashed, twelfths*

D. Do Not Set Off a Single Letter as a Syllable.

> **Wrong:** a-part, dough-y   **Right:** apart, doughy

65–67. Numbers

65. Generally, Write Out a Number in Words When

A. It Is a Single Digit:

> *six* hours, *two* athletes, *nine* members, *third* floor

B. It Is a Fraction Without a Whole Number:

> *one-tenth* of the voters; *three-fourths* full

But use numerals when a whole number precedes: The stock market fell $5^3/_8$ points.

C. It Begins a Sentence

> *Four hundred and fifty-two* people attended the concert.

Never begin a sentence with a numeral. If the number is a long one, rewrite the sentence to place the number elsewhere: Attendance at the concert was *1 287.*

66. Use Numerals in the Following Cases:

A. Any Number of Two Digits or More:

> *40* hours, *63* athletes, *600* members

Use spaces to separate every set of three digits (except in serial and telephone numbers, addresses, years in dates, and page numbers). Count from the right or the decimal point. Numbers of four digits only need not be spaced, but be consistent:

> *43 654* copies   *$2 383 949.96*
>
> *1 287* copies (or *1287* copies)
>
> A.D. *1066*   *2258* Ocean Road

Note: Some authorities recommend the use of commas as separators: *1,287* copies, *$2,383,949.96.* Whichever style you choose, be consistent.

Write very large round numbers as follows:

> *two million*   *23 million*   *4.2 trillion*

B. Numbers in These Special Uses:

Addresses	276 Fox Road	
Room Numbers	Room *217*	Suite *12*
Telephone Numbers	*459-7245*	*1-555-1212*
TV and Radio Stations	Channel *6*	
Chapter, Page, and Line Numbers	Chapter *7*	page *12*
Serial Numbers	XY307042	
Decimals and Percentages	*67.6*	*8* percent
Highway Numbers	Highway *403*	
Times	*5:02* a.m.	
Dates	May *10, 2001*	
Statistics, Scores	82 for; 47 against	Lions 7, Riders 7
Precise Measurements	6 by 3.2 cm	37.5° C
Other	Grade 3 Newsletter 23 Flight 117	Branch 546 Gate 7 Track 12

Note: Observe these cautions:

- Do not use ordinal numbers (*1st, first, 23rd, twenty-third*) between month and year in dates:

Wrong: March 15th, 2004

Right: March 15, 2004

Ordinal numbers are acceptable when month and day only are given. Use the numeral form when the day follows the month; use the written form when it precedes:

My birthday is March 15th.

He will be back in the office on the fifteenth of March.

- In formal writing, do not use the form *3/15/04* for a date.
- In specifying a time, use numerals with *a.m.* and *p.m.* and when emphasizing an exact time. Generally, use words otherwise:

3 p.m.	at 9:45 tomorrow
from 2:30 to 3:00 p.m.	the 8:02 train
four o'clock	around half-past five

- In measurements, write out the unit if writing out the number, if *using numerals, abbreviate the unit*:

6 cm x 3.2 cm	six metres	6 ft. 2 in.

C. Groups of Numbers in the Same Passage (do not mix words and numerals):

The control group's scores were *196, 57, 122, 10,* and *6.*

67. Write Amounts of Money as Follows:

A. Use Words to Express Approximate Amounts:

She makes about *a million dollars* a year.

B. Otherwise, Use Numerals:

29 or *$0.29* or *29 cents*

I earn *$9* an hour. *I earn $95.50* a day.

I won *$40, $30,* and *$5* at the races.

She won *$6* million. She won *$6.2* million. She won *6 889 346.45.*

68–69. Abbreviations

Abbreviations are intended mainly for limited spaces, such as signs, lists, and documentation. In ordinary writing, avoid abbreviations except for those listed in 68.

68. In Ordinary Writing, Abbreviate

A. Certain Titles Before Proper Names: *Mr., Mrs., Ms., Dr., St. (saint), Messrs., Mmes. . . . :*

Mr. Joel Sachs	*Mr.* Sachs	*Ms.* Wong
Mmes. Wong and Howe		
St. Teresa	*Rev.* Hector Gomez	*Hon.* Ida Ives

But write *Reverend* and *Honourable* in full if they follow *the:*

the *Reverend* Hector Gomez   the *Honourable* Ida Ives

Abbreviate military and civil titles unless you use only the person's last name:

Lt.-Col. Fabian Farley	*Sen.* Marc Lalonde
Lieutenant-Colonel Farley	*Senator* Lalonde

B. Degrees and Certain Other Titles After Proper Names: *Sr. (senior), Jr., Esq., M.A., Ph.D. . . . . :*

Ralph Grabowski, *Sr.,* visited Ramez Audi, *D.D.S.*

C. Certain Expressions Used with Numerals: *a.m., p.m., B.C., A.D., No. (number), $:*

9:30 *a.m.*   *A.D.* 1054   325 *B.C.*   *No.* 97   *$37.50*

Do not use such abbreviations without a numeral:

Wrong: She arrived this *a.m.*

Right: She arrived this *morning.*

Note: You may choose to write *B.C.E. (before the common era)* and *C.E. (common era)* instead of *B.C.* and *A.D. (A.D.* precedes the year; the others follow.) You may also choose to write any of these sets of initials without periods; whatever your choices, be consistent in style.

D. Certain Latin Phrases: *i.e., (that is), viz. (namely), e.g. (for example), cf. (compare), etc. (and so forth), vs. (versus).*

Note: Publishers tend to discourage the use of these abbreviations in the text of formal writing; you will do better to write out the English equivalents unless space is restricted (as in notes). Never write *and etc.;* it is redundant.

E. Certain Government Agencies and Other Well-Known Organizations (usually without periods): *RCMP, NASA, CSIS, CBC, IBM.* To be sure that your reader knows the meaning of such initials, give the full title at first mention, preferably followed by the initials in parentheses:

The *Canadian Automobile Association (CAA)* is campaigning for more highway funds. . . . Officials of the *CAA* are optimistic.

69. In Ordinary Writing, Do *Not* Abbreviate

A. Names of States, Countries, Months, Days, or Holidays:

Wrong: *Ont.* had a blizzard last *Tues., Xmas* Eve.

Right: *Ontario* had a blizzard last *Tuesday, Christmas Eve.*

B. Personal Names:

George (not *Geo.*) Woodcock wrote that.

C. The Words *Street, Avenue, Road, Park,* **and** *Company,* especially as part of proper names:

> *Wrong*: The Brooks *Co.* moved to Central *Av.*
>
> *Right:* The Brooks *Company* moved to Central *Avenue.*

D. The Word *and,* except in names of firms and in American Psychological Association reference-list citations:

> Ways *and* Means Committee; the Brooks *& Logan* Corporation. See 95C, page 61, for APA style.

E. References to a School Subject

> *Wrong:* The new *psych.* class is filled.
>
> *Right:* The new *psychology* class is filled.

F. The Words *Volume, Chapter,* **and** *Page,* except in documentation (see 95, pages 59–65), tabulations, and technical writing.

70–74. Spelling

To a reader, misspellings are the most obvious of writing errors, yet to the writer they are among the easiest to overlook. Do not trust a computer's spelling checker to do the job; most cannot tell *clam* from *calm* or *passed* from *past.* Rely on (1) using a reputable dictionary for words of which you are not sure and (2) very careful proofreadings—more than two or three. Proofread at least once backward, word for word from the end, so that the paper's flow of thought does not divert your mind from your proofreading task.

70. Spelling Improvement Techniques

A. Visualize the Correct Spelling of a Word. Look attentively at a word; then look away from it and try to see the printed word in your mind.

B. Practise Pronouncing Troublesome Words. Say each word aloud, syllable by syllable, a number of times.

ath-let-ic	quan-ti-ty	gov-ern-ment
ac-ci-den-tal-ly	di-sas-trous	e-quip-ment
val-u-a-ble	tem-per-a-ture	min-i-a-ture

C. Practise Writing Troublesome Words. Practise each word several times. Begin slowly and increase your speed until the correct form comes easily. You will need this drill to substitute correct spelling habits for faulty ones. Keep a corrected list of your misspelled words.

D. Distinguish Between Words Similar in Sound or Spelling. See 83, pages 48–52, for explanations of the following and many other such distinctions: *to/too/two, their/there/they're, its/it's, your/you're, loose/lose, whose/who's.*

E. Think of Related Words. Often you can determine whether to end a word with *-er* or *-ar, -ence* or *-ance, -able* or *-ible,* and so forth by thinking of a related form of the word. For example, if you think of *definition,* you can be fairly sure that *definite* ends in *-ite.* Examine these pairs:

famili**ari**ty	famili**ar**	aud**i**tion	aud**i**ble
gramm**ati**cal	gramm**ar**	stimul**a**tion	stimul**a**nt
peculi**ari**ty	peculi**ar**	symb**o**lic	symb**o**l
regul**ari**ty	regul**ar**	confid**e**ntial	confid**e**nt
imagin**a**tion	imagin**ar**y	exist**e**ntial	exist**e**nce
desper**a**tion	desper**a**te		

Exception: sensation—sensible, sensitive

F. Create and Use Memory Devices. Associate one word with another, find a word within a word, or make up jingles or nonsense sentences; such **mnemonics** can help you over the trouble spots in your problem words. Here are some examples:

> **Emma** is in a di**lemma**.
>
> She put a **dent** in the superinten**dent**.
>
> Station**ery** is pap**er**.
>
> A princi**ple** is a ru**le**.
>
> Poor *grammar* will m**ar** your writing.
>
> It is **vile** to have no pri**vile**ges.
>
> The ***villa*in** owns a **villa in** Spain.
>
> There is **a rat** in sepa**rat**e and in compa**rat**ive.
>
> I have **lice** on my **lice**nce!
>
> There is **iron** in the envi**ron**ment.
>
> There is a **meter** in the ce**meter**y.
>
> **Tim** has great op**tim**ism.
>
> With any *professor,* one **F** is enough.

Group words with similar characteristics, such as two sets of double letters (*accommodate, embarrass, possess*) or three *i*'s (*optimistic, primitive*) or names of occupations (*author, censor, conductor, emperor, investor, sponsor, professor*) or the three *-ceed* words (*proceed, exceed, succeed. All other words ending in the same sound are spelled with -cede, except supersede*).

71. The Five Basic Rules

A. The *ie* **Rule.** You probably know the old jingle:

> Put *i* before *e* except after *c,*
>
> Or when sounded like *a* as in *neighbour* and *weigh.*

That is, normally use *ie:*

ach**ie**ve	f**ie**ld	n**ie**ce
bel**ie**ve	gr**ie**f	rel**ie**ve
ch**ie**f	hyg**ie**ne	y**ie**ld
fr**ie**nd	misch**ie**f	misch**ie**vous

But after a *c*, use *ei:*

ceiling	de**cei**ve	re**cei**ve
con**cei**ve	per**cei**ve	re**cei**pt

Use *ei* also when the two letters sound like *AY:*

fr**ei**ght	n**ei**ghbour	v**ei**n
w**ei**gh	sl**ei**gh	h**ei**r

Actually, *ei* is usual when the two letters have any sound other than *EE: counterfeit, forfeit, foreign, height, neither,* (the British say *NYE-ther*), *leisure* (British *LEZZ-ure*).

> *Troublesome exceptions:* finan**cie**r, so**cie**ty, spe**cie**s; prot**ei**n, s**ei**ze, w**ei**rd.

B. The Final -*e* Rule: Drop a final silent *e* before a suffix beginning with a vowel (*a, e, i, o, u,* and here *y*):

write + ing = writing	fame + ous = famous
love + able = lovable	scare + y = scary
hope + ed = hoped	come + ing = coming
Exception: mileage	

But keep the *e* before a vowel suffix in these cases:

(1) *After c and g* (to keep a "soft" sound) before a suffix beginning with *a* or *o:* noti**ce/a**ble, chan**ge/a**ble, coura**ge/o**us, outra**ge/o**us, ven**ge/a**nce.

(2) *To avoid confusion with other words:* singe + ing = sing**e**/ing (to avoid confusion with singing); dye + ing = dy**e**/ing.

And keep the *e* when the suffix does not begin with a vowel: *hope/ful, love/less, lone/ly, safe/ty, state/ment, same/ness.* Exceptions: *judgment, argument, acknowledgment, truly, duly.*

C. The Final-*y* Rule: Change a final *y* to *i* before any suffix except *-ing:*

happy + ness = happiness	cry + ed = cried
busy + ly = busily	lady + es = ladies
cry/ing bury/ing	try/ing

But ignore this rule if a vowel precedes the *y:*

chimn**ey**/s	ann**oy**/ed	monk**ey**/s

Exceptions: lay, la**i**d; pay, pa**i**d; say, sa**i**d.

D. The Doubling Rule: Double a final consonant before a suffix beginning with a vowel (including *y*) if the original word does both of the following:

(1) *ends in consonant-vowel-consonant (cvc):*

cvc	cvc	cvc
drop, drop/**p**ing	bat, bat/**t**er	hum, hum/**m**able

(2) *and (if more than one syllable) is accented on the last syllable:*

cvc	cvc	cvc
oc**CUR**	oc**CUR**/**re**d	oc**CUR**/**re**nce
re**FER**	re**FER**/**re**d	re**FER**/**ra**l
be**GIN**	be**GIN**/**n**ing	be**GIN**/**n**er

Otherwise, do not double:

vvc	vvc	vcc
Not *cvc:* droop/ing,	preVAIL/ing,	dent/ed

Not accented on last syllable:

OFFer/ing, BENefit/ed, RECKon/ing

> **Note:** If the accent jumps back to an earlier syllable when the suffix is added, do not double: *conFER, CONfer/ence; reFER, REFer/ence.*

E. The Let-It-Alone Rule. When adding prefixes or suffixes or combining roots, do not add or drop letters unless you know that one of the spelling rules applies or that the word is irregular (see 74, page 43):

Prefix + Root	Root + Suffix	Root + Root
dis/appear	careful/ly	book/keeper
dis/satisfied	immediate/ly	grand/daughter
mis/spell	comical/ly	
re/commend	state/ment	
un/necessary	achieve/ment	

72. Forming Plurals.
To form most plurals, add *-s* to the singular (*toy, toys; dollar, dollars;* Donna *Remington,* the *Remingtons*). The following generalizations cover most other plurals. Consult your dictionary in other cases or when in doubt.

A. Add -*es* If You Hear an Added Syllable when you say a plural: *bush, bush/es; fox, fox/es; buzz, buzz/es; church, church/es.*

B. Add -*es* When the Final-*y* Rule Applies (see 71C, page 42): *sky, skies; liberty, liberties.*

C. Change Final *f* or *fe* to *v* and Add -*es* in the following and a few other similar nouns: *calf, calves; knife, knives; wife, wives; loaf, loaves; wharf, wharves; half, halves; life, lives.*

D. Add-es to Certain Singular Nouns Ending in *o*:

tomato, tomato**es**; potato, potato**es**; hero, hero**es**

With musical terms, with words having a vowel before the *o,* and with most other singular nouns ending in *o*, add just *-s:*

solo, solo**s**;   piano, piano**s**;   alto, alto**s**;

radio, radio**s**;   studio, studio**s**;   rodeo, rodeo**s**

With some words, you may use either -*s* or -*es:*

domino, domino**s**, domino**es**;   zero, zero**s**, zero**es**

Consult a dictionary for other final -*o* word plurals.

E. Change Final -*is* to -*es* in Many Words:

basis, bas**es**; synopsis, synops**es**; oasis, oas**es**;

hypothesis, hypothes**es**; thesis, thes**es**; axis, ax**es**;

parenthesis, parenthes**es**; analysis, analys**es**; crisis, cris**es**

F. Make Compound Words Plural as Follows:

(1) With solid (unhyphenated) compounds, add the
-s *to the very end:* cupfuls, *mouthfuls*

(2) With hyphenated compounds, add the -s *to the*
noun: fathers-in-law, *passers-by*

G. Use the Foreign Plural for Some Nouns of Foreign
Origin: *alumnus, alumni (male); alumna, alumnae (female);*
stimulus, stimuli; stratum, strata; curriculum, curricula.

With many other such nouns, you may use either the
foreign or English plural:

radius, radi**i** or radius**es**; stadium, stadi**a** or
stadium**s**; octopus, octop**i** or octopus**es**; index,
ind**ices** or index**es**; appendix, appendi**ces** or
appendix**es**; antenna, antenn**ae** (of insects) or
antenna**s** (of electronic devices); phenomenon,
phenomen**a** or phenomenon**s**; criterion, criteri**a** or
criterion**s**; vertebra, vertebr**ae** or vertebra**s**.

Many of these use the foreign plural in scholarly or technical
writing and the English plural in general writing. Your
dictionary may specify when each should be used.

Note: Remember that *criteria, phenomena,* and *media* are plurals
and require plural verbs. Most authorities also consider *data*
plural in formal English. For the singular, use *body of data,* or, if
appropriate, *database.*

H. For Clarity, Use -'s for Plurals of Letters and Symbols

Optimistic has three *i*'**s**. [not *three is*]

See 41B, page 30.

73. Non-standard and Alternative Spellings

A. Avoid Non-standard Spellings, such as *nite, lite, rite* (for
right), and *thru,* which occur mostly in product names. Do not
use them elsewhere.

B. Use Preferred Spellings. Some words have alternative
correct spellings: *programmer, programer; kidnapper,*

kidnaper; dialogue, dialog; catalogue, catalog. When the
dictionary lists two or more spellings, you are safer using the
first, which is considered preferred.

74. 100 Problem Words

Many bothersome spelling words have been explained in the
suggestions and rules above. Others, pairs of look-alikes or
sound-alikes such as *advice* and *advise,* are clarified in 83,
pages 48–52. Below are 100 more "demons."

absence	approximately	conscientious
acknowledge	argument	courteous
acquaintance	article	criticism
acquire	auxiliary	criticize
across	business	curiosity
adolescence	calendar	definite
amateur	category	description
analysis	committee	desperate
apologize	competent	develop
apparent	condemn	discipline
doesn't	guidance	management
eighth	height	manoeuvre
erroneous	hindrance	mathematics
exaggerate	hypocrisy	meant
excellent	independent	memento
existence	indispensable	mischievous
fascinating	irrelevant	necessary
forty	irresistible	ninety
fulfill	knowledge	ninth
guarantee	maintenance	nucleus
omission	personally	restaurant
opinion	playwright	rhythm
opportunity	prejudice	ridiculous
parallel	prevalent	sacrifice
particularly	procedure	schedule
perform	psychology	secretary
permanent	pursue	sensible
permissible	questionnaire	sincerely
perseverance	reminisce	souvenir
persistent	repetition	supposed to
suppression	tragedy	unusually
surprise	truly	used to
synonym	twelfth	vacuum
tendency		

SECTIONS 80–83 Word Choice

The clarity, style, and tone of your writing, and its acceptance by your audience, depend largely on your choice of words.

80. Be Concise, Clear, and Original.

A large vocabulary is an asset, but using too many "big words" can weaken your writing. Use words not to impress but to convey meaning accurately, clearly, concisely, and with originality.

A. Cut Needless Words.

(1) Redundancy (needless repetition) in general:

Wordy: *In* the first chapter *of the book, for all intents and purposes, it* sets the scene *for the future* events to come *in the book. In my opinion, I think that* the *large* purple mansion, garish *in colour,* is an *absolutely* perfect setting for mysterious *happenings and occurrences.*

Concise: The first chapter sets the scene. The garish purple mansion is a perfect setting for mysterious events to come.

Caution: Not all repetition is redundancy. Sometimes you must repeat for clarity or emphasis.

Unclear: The three computer programs contained several innovations. The first attracted the most attention. [first program or first innovation?]

Clear: The three computer programs contained several innovations. The first program attracted the most attention.

(2) Double negatives, double subjects, and double that: `ESL`

They *had* (not *hadn't*) hardly enough for survival. [*Hardly, barely,* and *scarcely* mean *almost not* and thus act as negatives.]

After the trial the lawyer ~~she~~ congratulated us.

The editorial claimed *that,* despite the nationwide decrease in crime, ~~that~~ our city was unsafe.

B. Purge Overblown Diction. Use plain, direct wording. It is generally clearer and carries more force than elaborate language. Avoid filling your writing with words ending in *-ion, -ity, -ment,* or *-ize,* such as *situation* or *utilize.* Examples:

Overblown	Concise
crisis situation	crisis
make a decision	decide
underwent a conversion	converted
determine the veracity of	verify
attain the lunar surface	reach the moon
utilize the emergency audible warning system	press the alarm button

Overblown and obscure: Implementation of federally mandated reorganization procedures within designated departments, with the objective of downsizing, is anticipated in the near future. It is the company's intention to attempt the consequent organizational framework adjustments with minimal negative impact upon company personnel.

Concise and clear: Our company must soon begin federally ordered cutbacks in some departments, but we intend to do so with the fewest layoffs possible. [This version gains force also by using active voice *(we intend)* instead of passive *(is anticipated).* See 15B, page 9.]

Gear your vocabulary to your intended audience. Do not talk down to them, but do not talk over their heads either. Avoid *jargon* (technical or other terms unknown to most general readers, such as *multi-modality approach to ESL*) unless your audience are specialists in the subject. If you must use such a term, define it in parentheses following its first use.

Here are some common expressions that can be pared down:

Redundant, Wordy or Overblown	Concise
absolutely perfect, **very** unique	perfect, unique [see17B, page 12]
maintenance **activity**	maintenance
actual fact, true fact	fact
and etc.	etc. [see 81, pages 45–47]
Where is the car **at**?	Where is the car?
at this (that) point in time	now (then)
on the **basis of** this report	from this report
but yet, but however	but *or* yet *or* however
each and every	*use only one:* each *or* every
in the **event that**	if
residential **facility**	residential building, home
the **fact that** she had no cash; **due to the fact that** he knew; **except for the fact that** it was void	her lack of cash; because he knew; except that it was void
take the rainfall **factor** into consideration	consider rainfall
general consensus of opinion	consensus
generally (*or* **usually**) always	always *or* generally *or* usually
that **kind** (*or* **sort**) **of a** man	that kind (*or* sort) of man
jumped **off of** the wall	jumped off the wall

continue **on**	(*usually*) continue
Meet me **outside of** the house.	Meet me outside the house.
Their romance is **over with.**	Their romance is over.
the registration **procedure,** the education **process**	registration, education
for the **purpose of** studying	to study; for studying
The **reason** they died **was because** no help came	They died because no help came.
They know the **reason why** he lied.	They know why he lied.
refer back to	refer to
in (with) regard(s) to this matter	about (*or* concerning) this matter
round **in shape**; blue **in colour**; 210 cm tall **in height**	round; blue; 210 cm tall
The crime **situation** is improving.	Crime is down.
My financial **situation** is very poor.	I have little money.
connect **up**; road ends **up**; climb **up**; meet **up with**	connect; ends; climb; meet
She got good **usage** from her car. She **utilized** her cell phone to call home.	good use; used her cell phone. Usage *means "customary use,"* as in English usage. Utilize is *for special uses*: Ground-up glass is utilized for paving.

C. Be Specific. A **general** term covers a wide grouping: *disease, music, science*. A **specific** term singles out one of that grouping: *malaria, "Four Strong Winds," archaeology.* (Of course, there may be intermediate terms: music → song → folk song → "Four Strong Winds.")

Sometimes you must generalize, as in topic and summary sentences:

> The nation has seen urban crime decrease markedly.

But to avoid vagueness, you need, in accompanying sentences, specifics that will support your generalization:

> Murder is down by half and sexual assault by 20 percent.

(See 91B, pages 53–54, for examples in paragraphs.) Be as specific as your context allows: a *reddish purple* (not *colourful*) sunset; *two dozen* (not *many*) onlookers; his *dazzling whirls and leaps* (not his *fine dancing*).

General or Vague	**More Specific**
many, a number of, some, a lot of	more than 100, about 40 000, fewer than 20, nearly half . . .

thing	item, detail, article, idea, deed, quality, event, incident, point (*for thing she said*), foods (*for things to eat*), sights (*for things to see*) . . .
fine, nice, wonderful, great	sunny, friendly, considerate, record-setting, inspiring

D. Use Fresh, Original Wording.

(1) Avoid trite, overused expressions (clichés), such as *last but not least,* which bore readers and signal your lack of originality. Be suspicious of expressions that pop too readily into your mind—they may well be clichés. Watch also for words you tend to use too often, such as *very* (try *quite, rather,* or *extremely*; or better, specify a degree: not *very cold* but *so cold that our eyelids froze*).

Some Common Clichés to Avoid

add insult to injury	my mind was a blank
better late than never	quick as a wink
between a rock and a hard place	raining cats and dogs
down but not out	soft as silk
easier said than done	time flew by
hungry as a horse	tried and true
in this day and age	water under the bridge

(2) Use imaginative language. For originality, create some imaginative comparisons—**similes** and **metaphors:**

> **Simile** (uses *like* or *as*): Earning a Ph.D. is *like climbing Everest barefoot.*

> **Metaphor:** The subway train, *a red-eyed dragon,* roared into the station.

E. Consider Connotation. *Thrifty, frugal, stingy,* and *parsimonious* all refer to holding on to one's money, but each has a different **connotation**, or implied meaning: you would convey a negative rather than a positive connotation if you used *parsimonious* instead of *thrifty*.

81. Maintain the Appropriate Language Level.
Some words and expressions are considered unsuitable for formal writing (such as a research paper) and speaking (such as a graduation address).

Among these are

- **Colloquialisms** (used only in informal, casual conversation or writing intending a casual tone). Included among colloquialisms are shortened forms of words, such as *exam, prof, chem, ID* (for *identification*):

  Colloquial (informal): The chem prof ID's everyone before the exam.

Formal: The chemistry professor checks everyone's identification before the examination.

- **Regionalisms** and **dialect words** (known only within certain geographic areas or population groups): *pop* (for *soft drink*), *leastways, that's a hoot.*

- **Slang** (used only among certain social groups, such as teenagers). Most slang fades fast, and thus may be unknown to many readers. Who today refers to a *gat* or a *lug*?

  Slang: He must have paid *some heavy bread* for digs like that.

  Standard: He must have paid *plenty of money* for a *house* like that.

- **Non-standard** (ungrammatical) expressions (always to be avoided): *ain't got no* money

Note: The lines separating colloquial, slang, and non-standard expressions are sometimes blurry: authorities may differ, or words may over time slide up or down the acceptability scale. Moreover, there is no sharp line dividing formal and informal: the *National Post's* sports pages are less formal than a scholarly journal article. Consider the following list as guidelines rather than ironclad rules.

Common Expressions Not Suitable in Formal Writing
[Most are colloquial. Regionalisms are labelled (R), non-standard terms (N).]

alright. Say *all right.*

red **and/or** green. (Acceptable in legal and business writing but not in general formal writing; also sometimes unclear.) Say *green, red, or both.*

anyways, anywheres, everywheres, nowheres, somewheres (N). Say *anyway or any way, anywhere, everywhere. . . .*

aren't I. Say *am I not.*

awful. Say *quite bad, ugly, shocking. . . .*

awful(ly) good. Say *quite, very, extremely.* See 16A, page 11.

want it **badly.** Say *greatly, very much.*

being as (how), being that. Say *because, since.*

you **better** do it. Say *you had better, you'd better.*

between you and I, for him and I. . . . After a preposition say *you and me, him and me.* See 19C, page 14.

a **bunch** of people. Say *group, crowd.*

I **bust, busted, bursted** balloons (N). Say *I burst balloons* (present and past), *I have burst balloons.*

He had no doubt **but that (but what)** she knew it. Say *He had no doubt that.*

can't hardly (scarcely, barely). Say *can hardly, scarcely, barely.* See 80A(2), page 44.

can't help but love you. Say *can't help loving you.*

Contact me tomorrow. Say *Call, See, E-mail. . . .* (Some authorities do accept the verb *contact* in formal usage, to mean "get in touch with." *Contact* as a noun is acceptable formally.)

cop(s). Say *police officer, police.*

could of, may of, might of, must of, should of, would of, ought

to of (N). Say *could have, may have, might have . . .* or, informally, *could've, may've, might've. . . .*

a couple of friends, days, problems. . . . Say *two friends, three days, several problems. . . .* Save *couple* for a joined pair, such as *an engaged couple.*

Due to the time, we left. Say *Because of the time. . . .* (*Due to* is acceptable after *be* or *seem: The delay was due to rain.* See 80B, pages 44–45.)

He **enthused (was enthused)** about it. Say *He was enthusiastic about it.*

reading Munro, Atwood, **etc.** In paragraph writing, say *and others* or *and so forth,* or say *reading writers such as Munro and Atwood.*

every bit as old as. Say *just as old as.*

every so often, every once in a while. Say *occasionally, from time to time.*

every which way. Say *every way.*

She has a **funny** accent. Say *peculiar, odd.*

If I **had of** known (N). Say *had known.*

He **had ought** to go (N). Say *He ought to.*

a half a page. Say *a half page, half a page.*

They **have got** the answer. Say *have the answer.*

hisself, ourselfs, yourselfs, themself(s), theirself(s), theirselves (N). Say *himself, ourselves, yourselves, themselves.*

Hopefully, the bus will come. Say *We hope the bus will come.* (Strictly, *hopefully* means "full of hope." The bus is not full of hope.)

if and when I go. Generally, say either *if I go* or *when I go.*

Sinatra's music **impacted (on)** three generations. Say *greatly affected, influenced, brought happiness to. . . . Impact* as a noun (a great *impact*) is acceptable.

irregardless (N). Say *regardless.*

is when, is where. See 27E, page 24.

It being late, we left. Say *Since it was* or *Because it was.* See 26A, pages 21–22.

kid(s). Say *child(ren).*

kind of (sort of) soft. Say *rather soft, somewhat soft,* or just *soft.*

a lot (often misspelled *alot*) **of, lots of.** Say *much, many;* better, say *fifty* or *dozens of.* See 80C, page 45.

mad at you. Say *angry with you. Mad* means "insane."

most all the books. Say *almost all.*

nowhere near ready. Say *not nearly ready.*

O.K., OK, okay. Say *all right, correct* (adj.); *approval* (noun); *approve* (verb).

everyone **outside of** John. Say *except John.*

plan on going. Say *plan to go.*

plenty good. Say *quite good.* (*Plenty* is acceptable as a noun: *plenty of fish.*)

I'm going, **plus** Nan. He felt sick; **plus,** he had no money. Say *Nan and I are going. He felt sick; besides (also, moreover), he had no money.*

a **pretty** sum; a **pretty** long ride. Say *a very large sum, a fairly long ride.*

real good, **real** smooth. Say *very, quite.*

seeing as how, seeing that. Say *since, because.*

It **seldom ever** changed. Say *seldom* or *never, seldom if ever, hardly ever.*

in bad **shape.** Say *in poor condition.*

They were **so** happy. Say *They were so happy that they wept.* See 27C, page 24.

She ran **so** she could stay fit. Say *so that she could.*

The bill was vague, **so** the court struck it down. (Frequently joining independent clauses with *so* gives your writing an informal tone. Try recasting the sentence: *The court struck down the bill because it was vague.*)

Woods is **some** golfer! He worried **some.** Say *Woods is quite a golfer! He worried somewhat or a little.*

It was **such** a loud noise. There is **no such a** place. Say *such a loud noise that her ears hurt* [see 27C, page 24]. *There is no such place.*

This would **sure** help. Say *surely help.* See 16A, page 11.

terribly sad, a **terrific** win. Say *extremely sad, a last-minute win, an exciting win.*

them weapons (N). Say *those weapons.*

these kind (sort, type), those kind. Say *this kind, that kind, this sort, that type.* (*Kind, type,* and *sort* are singular; they must take singular modifiers. For plurals say *these kinds, those types,* etc.

this (these) here, that (those) there (N). Say *this, that, these, those.*

Try and win. Be **sure and** vote. Say *Try to win. Be sure to vote.*

It was **very** appreciated. Say *very much, greatly.*

Jones read in the newspaper **where** Smith had died (N). Say *that Smith had died.*

If *Seinfield* **would have** continued, it **would have** stayed popular (N). See 14B(7), page 8.

Keep your language level consistent within a paper. Determine the right tone for each of your writings from its nature (research paper, informal essay, chatty letter), its purpose (to amuse, to arouse to action, to stimulate thought), and its intended audience. Be especially alert for colloquial expressions creeping into your formal papers.

82. Use Non-discriminatory Terms. `ESL`

A. Non-sexist Terms. A word or expression is considered sexist if it wrongly excludes, diminishes, or denigrates the role of one sex (usually women) in its context: *A buyer should shop around for the car he wants. The postman is here.* [Women too buy cars and deliver mail.] *They sent a lady plumber.* [*Lady* seems to imply that women are not expected to be plumbers or that they are not good ones.] You can avoid sexist usage as follows:

(1) Pronouns. The traditional use of *he, his,* and *him* in contexts applicable to both sexes (Every *student* needs *his* calculator) is now widely regarded as sexist.

Substituting for these pronouns may present a problem, however, because English lacks common-gender equivalents. Try either of the following solutions, taking care to preserve clarity and consistency with context:

- *Shift to the plural where possible:* Buyers should shop around for the cars *they* want. All *students* need *their* calculators.
- *Remove gender where possible:* Shopping around for a car will ensure a good buy. Student calculators are required. A worker's attitude affects ~~his~~ job performance.

Other solutions are less satisfactory. Using *he or she, his or her, her or him* (Every student needs *his or her* calculator) sounds clumsy after a number of repetitions. Substituting *you* or *your* (in that class *you* need a calculator) is colloquial. Using *they, their, them* with a singular noun (Every *student* needs *their* calculator), though common colloquially, is generally not accepted in formal English.

(2) Nouns. Where both sexes are or may be included, replace single-sex nouns with gender-neutral ones:

Single-sex	Inclusive
mankind	humankind
seaman	sailor
policeman	(police) officer
postman	letter carrier
fireman	firefighter
repairman	repairer
housewife	homemaker
waitress	server
the average man	the average person

Use *ladies* only as a parallel to *gentlemen.* Omit *lady* or (generally) *woman* before *pilot, engineer,* and the like. Refer to females 16 and older as *(young) women,* not *girls.* Avoid expressions that put women in a lower category, such as *farmers and their wives* [the wives work the farm, too; say just *farmers* or *farm families*], *man and wife* [say *husband and wife*].

B. Other Non-discriminatory Terms

(1) Ethnic, racial, religious. Avoid ethnic stereotypes and negative terms such as, *half-breed, redneck, culturally deprived.* Avoid terms that place Europe at the centre of the world (say *East Asian,* not *Far Eastern* [that is, far east of Europe] or *Oriental*) or that cast one race as dominant: *non-white* may imply that white is the racial standard; *flesh-coloured*—meaning white flesh—ignores most of the world; words that equate black with bad (*a black mark, blacklist*) imply black Canadian racial inferiority. Call racial, national,

ethnic, and religious groups by the names they prefer: *Black Canadians, First Nations, Native Canadians, Inuit* (not *Eskimos*). Omit hyphens in terms such as *Italian Canadian* and *Chinese Canadian*. Do not label a religion a cult; say *house of worship,* not *church* (unless referring specifically to Christians).

*(2) **Disabilities.*** Avoid calling persons with disabilities *crippled, deformed,* or the like; focus on the person, not the impairment: *a wheelchair user,* not *an amputee; a person with a mental disorder,* not *a mental case.*

83. Distinguish Between Similar Words. Below
are sets of two (or more) words that may cause confusion because of their similar appearance, sound, spelling, or meaning. The "big ten," the most common trouble sets, are highlighted in grey type.

a, an. See 16E(1), page 11.

accept, except. *Accept* (verb) means "to receive": The Bare Naked Ladies *accepted* the Juno Award.

Except (usually preposition) means "excluding": Peace prevailed in all Europe *except* the Balkans.

Note: *Except* is occasionally a verb, meaning "to exclude": The judge told the lawyers to *except* the disputed testimony from their summation.

adapt, adopt. *Adapt* means "to adjust or make suitable": She *adapted* her office to accommodate computers.

Adopt means "to take as one's own": She *adopted* the jargon of computer hackers. They *adopted* a girl.

advice, advise. *Advice* (noun) means "counsel": I was skeptical of the salesperson's *advice.*

Advise (verb) means "to give advice": The salesperson *advised* me to buy the larger size.

affect, effect. Most commonly, affect (verb) means "to have an effect on": Mostly, the disease affected poor people.

Most commonly, *effect* (noun) means "a result, consequence, outcome": The disease had a devastating *effect* on the poor.

Note: Less commonly, *affect* (as a verb) means "to pretend or imitate": He *affected* a British accent. *Effect* (as a verb) means "to accomplish, to bring about": The medicine *effected* a cure.

afterward, afterwards. Use either; be consistent.

aisle, isle. An *aisle* is a passage between rows of seats: the side *aisle.*

An *isle* is an island: the Emerald *Isle.*

all ready, already. *All ready* means "fully ready": the runner was *all* [fully] *ready* for the marathon.

Already means "previously" or "by this time": Karl had *already* crossed the finish line.

all together, altogether. *All together* means "in a group": We were *all together* at the reunion.

Altogether means "wholly, completely": I was *altogether* surprised at the score.

allusion, illusion, delusion. *Allusion means* "an indirect reference": The play has many Biblical *allusions.*

Illusion means "a temporary false perception or a magic trick": It was an optical *illusion.*

Delusion refers to a lasting false perception or belief about oneself or other persons or things: He had the *delusion* of expecting success without effort.

among. See *between.*

amoral, immoral. *Amoral* means "not concerned with morality": An infant's acts are *amoral.*

Immoral means "against morality": Murder is *immoral.*

amount, number. *Amount* refers to things in bulk or mass: a large *amount* of grain; no *amount* of persuasion.

Number refers to countable objects: a *number* of books.

ante-, anti-. Both are prefixes. *Ante-* means "before": *anteroom, antedate, antecedent.*

Anti- means "against": *antibody, anti-social, antidote.*

anxious, eager. *Anxious* conveys worry or unease: Forecasters grew *anxious* about the oncoming storm.

Eager conveys strong desire: They were *eager* to marry.

any more, anymore. *Any more* means "additional": Is there *any more* fuel? There isn't *any more.*

Anymore means "at present" or "any longer": He doesn't write home *anymore.*

any one, anyone. *Any one* refers to any single item of a number of items: You may take *any one* of these courses.

Anyone means "any person": Has *anyone* here seen Kelly?

apt, likely, liable. *Apt* refers to probability based on normal, habitual, or customary tendency: He was *apt* to throw things when frustrated.

Likely indicates mere probability: It is *likely* to rain.

Liable, strictly, refers to legal responsibility: Jaywalkers are *liable* to arrest. Informally, it is used also with any undesirable or undesired risk: He's *liable* to get into trouble.

as, because, since. For expressing cause, *because* is most precise; *since* and *as* may ambiguously convey either time or cause: *Since* he's been put in charge, three people have quit.

Note: Although many schoolchildren have been told never to begin a sentence with *because,* it is quite all right to do so—as long as you avoid a fragment.

as, like. See *like.*

awhile, a while. Do not use the adverb *awhile* after *for* or *in.* One may stay *awhile* (adverb), stay a *while* (noun), stay for a *while* (noun), but not for *awhile* (adverb).

bad, badly. See 16C, page 11.

because. See *as, because, since.*

beside, besides. *Beside* (preposition) means "at the side of": My lawyer stood *beside* me [at my side] in court.

Besides (preposition, conjunctive adverb) means "other than" or "in addition (to)": *Besides* me, only my lawyer knew. My lawyer is clever; *besides,* she is experienced.

between, among. *Between* implies *two* persons or things in a relationship; *among* implies *three* or more: Emissaries shuttled *between* London and Moscow. A dispute arose *among* the four nations.

born, borne. Use *born* (with *be*) only to mean "have one's birth": They *were born* [had their birth] in Brazil.

Use *borne* before *by* and elsewhere: The baby was *borne by* a surrogate mother. She has *borne* two sons. Zullo has *borne* the burdens of office well.

brake, break. *Brake* refers to stopping: Apply the *brake. Brake* the car carefully.

Break refers to destroying, damaging, exceeding, or interrupting: Don't *break* the glass. I'll *break* the record. Take a 10-minute *break*.

bring, take. In precise usage, *bring* means "to come (here) with," and *take* means "to go (there) with": *Take* this cheque to the bank, and *bring* back the cash.

can, may. In formal usage, *can* means "to be able to" (They *can* solve any equation), and *may* means "to have permission to" (You *may* leave now). *May* also expresses possibility: It *may* snow tonight.

canvas, canvass. A *canvas* is a cloth: Buy a *canvas* tent. *Canvass* means "to solicit": *Canvass* the area for votes.

capitol, capital. Use *capitol* for the building where a legislature meets: The Vermont's governor's office is in the *capitol*.

Elsewhere, use *capital*: Victoria is the provincial *capital* [seat of government]. The firm has little *capital* [money]. It was a *capital* [first-rate] idea. Murder can be a *capital* offence [one punishable by death].

carat, caret, carrot. Gold and gems are weighed in *carats*.

A *caret* (∧) signals an omission: I ∧ going home.

A *carrot* is a vegetable: Eat your *carrots*.

casual, causal. *Casual* means "occurring by chance, informal, unplanned"; *causal* means "involving cause."

censor, censure. To *censor* is to examine written, visual, recorded, or broadcast material to delete objectionable content: Many parents want to *censor* violent television shows.

To *censure* is to criticize or blame: The senator was *censured* for unethical conduct.

cite, site, sight. *Cite* means "to quote an authority or give an example": Did you *cite* all your sources in the paper?

Site means "location": Here is the new building *site*.

Sight refers to seeing: The ship's lookout *sighted* land. Use your *sight* and hearing.

classic, classical. *Classic* means "of the highest class or quality": *Hamlet* is a *classic* play.

Classical means "pertaining to the art and life of ancient Greece and Rome": *Classical* Greek art idealized the human figure.

Classical music refers to symphonies and the like.

coarse, course. *Coarse* means "rough, not fine": *coarse* wool.

A *course* is a path or a series of lessons: race *course*, art *course*.

compare to, compare with. *Compare to* means "to liken, to point out one or more similarities": Earning a Ph.D. has been *compared to* climbing Everest barefoot.

Compare with means "to examine to determine similarities and differences": The report *compares* United States medical care *with* that of Canada.

compliment, complement. *Compliment* means "to express praise": The dean *complimented* Harris on her speech.

Complement means "to complete, enhance, or bring to perfection": The illustrations should *complement* the text.

The nouns *compliment* and *complement* are distinguished similarly. Free tickets are *complimentary*.

comprise, compose, include. Strictly, *comprise* means "to be made up of (in entirety)": Our university *comprises* eight colleges.

Compose means "to make up, to constitute": Eight colleges *compose* our university. Our university is *composed* of eight colleges.

Include means "to contain (but not necessarily in entirety)": Our university *includes* colleges of business and pharmacy.

continual, continuous. *Continual* means "frequently repeated": She worked in spite of *continual* interruptions.

Continuous means "without interruption": The explorers could hear the *continuous* roar of the falls.

convince, persuade. *Convince* emphasizes changing a person's belief: *Convince* me of your sincerity.

Persuade emphasizes moving a person to action: The activist *persuaded* bystanders to join the protest.

correspond to, correspond with. *Correspond to* means "to be similar or analogous to": The German gymnasium *corresponds to* the Canadian private high school.

Correspond with means "to be in agreement or conformity with": His behaviour did not *correspond with* our rules. It also means "to communicate with by exchange of letters."

council, counsel, consul. *Council* means "a deliberative assembly": The Parish *Council* debated the issue.

Counsel (noun) means "advice" or "attorney": He sought the *counsel* of a psychologist. She is the *counsel* for the defence.

Counsel (verb) means "to advise": They *counselled* us to wait before marrying.

Consul means "an officer in the foreign service": The distinguished guest was the *consul* from Spain.

credible, credulous, creditable. *Credible* means "believable": A witness's testimony must be *credible*.

Credulous means "too ready to believe; gullible": A *credulous* person is easily duped.

Creditable means "praiseworthy": The young pianist gave a *creditable* performance of a difficult work.

decent, descent. *Decent* means "proper, right": This is not a *decent* film for children.

Descent means "a going down" or "ancestry": The plane's *descent* was bumpy. He's of Guyanese *descent*.

delusion. See *allusion*.

device, devise. A *device* (noun) is an invention or a piece of equipment: This *device* turns the lights on at dusk.

To *devise* (verb) is to invent: *Devise* a new mousetrap.

different from, different than. Formal usage requires *different from*: His paper is hardly *different from* yours.

Note: Different than is gaining acceptance when introducing a clause: The scores were *different* than we expected (smoother than *different from* what).

differ from, differ with. *Differ from* expresses unlikeness: His paper *differs* greatly *from* mine.

Differ with expresses divergence of opinion: The Prime Minister *differed with* the premiers regarding transfer payments.

disinterested, uninterested. *Disinterested* means "not influenced by personal interest; impartial, unbiased": A *disinterested* judge gives fair rulings.

Uninterested means simply "not interested": The *uninterested* judge dozed on the bench.

dived, dove. *Dived* is the preferred past tense and past participle of *dive*: The pelicans *dived* (not *dove*) into the sea.

each other, one another. *Each other* refers to *two* persons or things; *one another*, to *three or more*.

eager. See *anxious*.

effect. See *affect.*

emigrate, immigrate. *Emigrate* means "to leave a country"; *immigrate* means "to enter a new country": Millions *emigrated* from Europe. They *immigrated* to North America.

eminent, imminent. *Eminent* means "distinguished": She's an *eminent* surgeon.
Imminent means "about to happen": Rain is *imminent.*

ensure, insure. *Ensure* is preferred for "make sure, guarantee": to *ensure* your safety, wear seat belts.
Insure refers to insurance (protection against loss): *Insure* your valuables.

envelop, envelope. To *envelop* is to surround: Fog *envelops* us.
An *envelope* holds a letter: Seal the *envelope.*

every one, everyone. Use *everyone* wherever you can substitute *everybody*: Everyone (everybody) left early.
Elsewhere, use *every one* (usually followed by *of*): Every one of the flights was delayed.

except. See *accept.*

famous, notable, notorious. *Famous* means "widely known": it usually has favourable connotations.
Notable means "worthy of note" or "prominent"; a person can be *notable* without being *famous.*
Notorious means "widely known in an unfavourable way": Clifford Olsen is a *notorious* killer.

farther, further. *Farther* refers to physical distance: Roadblocks kept the troops from going *farther.*
Further means "to a greater extent or degree": The UN decided to discuss the issue *further.*

fewer, less. *Fewer* refers to number; use it with countable things: *Fewer* lakes are polluted these days.
Use *less* with things that are not countable but are considered in bulk or mass: *Less* wheat grew this year.

formally, formerly. *Formally* means "according to proper form": Introduce us *formally.*
Formerly means "previously": They *formerly* lived here.

former, latter; first, last. *Former* and *latter* refer to the first and second named of only two items: Concerning jazz and rock, she prefers the *former* [jazz], but he prefers the *latter* [rock]. In a series of three or more, use *first* and *last.*

forth, fourth. *Forth* means "forward": Go *forth* and conquer. *Fourth* is 4th: They visited American friends on the *Fourth* of July.

good, well. See 16C, page 11.

hanged, hung. Strict usage requires *hanged* when you mean "executed": She was *hanged* as a spy.
Elsewhere, use *hung.* They *hung* the flag high.

healthy, healthful. *Healthy* means "possessing health": The children are *healthy.*
Healthful means "conducive to health": Bran is *healthful.*

historic, historical. Strictly, *historic* means "famous or important in history": July 1, 1867, is an *historic* date.
Historical means "pertaining to history": Good *historical* novels immerse us in their times.

if, whether. When presenting alternatives, use *whether* for precision: Tell us *whether* (not *if*) you pass or fail. Also, drop an unneeded *or not* after *whether:* He was unsure *whether* ~~or not~~ to go.

illusion. See *allusion.*

immigrate. See *emigrate.*

imminent. See *eminent.*

immoral. See *amoral.*

imply, infer. Writers or speakers *imply* (state indirectly or suggest): The union's statement *implied* that the management was lying.
Readers or listeners *infer* (draw a conclusion or derive by reasoning): From these data we *infer* that a recession is near.

in, into. Use *into* with movement from outside to inside: The nurse ran *into* Wilcox's room.
Elsewhere, use *in:* Wilcox lay quietly *in* his bed.

include. See *comprise.*

incredible, incredulous. A fact or happening is *incredible* (unbelievable): Astronomical distances are *incredible.*
A person is *incredulous* (unbelieving): He was *incredulous* when told how far the Milky Way extends.

individual, person, party. Do not use *party or individual* when you mean simply *person:* They heard from a certain *person* (not *individual* or *party*) that she was engaged. Except in legal and telephone-company usage, and when you mean "one taking part," do not use *party* to refer to one person.
Use *individual* only when emphasizing a person's singleness: Will you act with the group or as an *individual?*

ingenious, ingenuous. *Ingenious* means "clever"; *ingenuous* means "naive, having childlike frankness": *Ingenious* swindlers forged a surveyor's report about the gold and sold stock to *ingenuous* investors.

instance, instants, instant's. *Instance* means "a case or example": She noted each *instance* of violence. [plural: *instances*]
Instants is the plural of instant, meaning "a brief time, a particular moment": She did it in a few *instants.*
Instant's is the possessive of *instant:* They came at an *instant's* notice.

insure. See *ensure.*

isle. See *aisle.*

its, it's. *Its* is the possessive of *it:* The dog wagged *its* tail.
It's is the contraction of *it is.* Use *it's* only if you can correctly substitute *it is* in your sentence: *It's* (*it is*) ready.

last, latter. See *former.*

later, latter. *Later,* the comparative from of *late,* means "more late."
For latter, see former.

lay. See *lie.*

lead, led. *Lead* (rhymes with *need*) is the present tense of the verb meaning "to conduct, to go at the head of, to show the way": Browne can *lead* us to prosperity.
Led is the past tense and past participle of the same verb: Browne (has) *led* us to prosperity.
Lead (rhymes with *dead*) is a metal: I need a *lead* pipe.

learn, teach. *Learn* means "to acquire knowledge": Toddlers must *learn* not to touch electrical outlets.
Teach means "to impart knowledge": Parents must *teach* toddlers not to touch electrical outlets.

leave, let. *Leave* means "to depart": I must *leave* now.
Let means "to permit": *Let* me go.

less. See *fewer.*

lessen, lesson. To *lessen* is to diminish: His pain *lessened*.
A *lesson* is a unit of learning: Study your *lesson*.

liable, likely. See *apt*.

lie, lay. *Lie* means "to rest" and is an intransitive verb (it never takes an object): Don't *lie* on the new couch. The islands *lie* under the tropical sun. Here *lies* Jeremiah Todd.
Lay means "to put, to place" and is a transitive verb (it must take an object): *Lay* your *head* on this pillow. Let me *lay* your *fears* to rest.
To complicate matters, the past tense of *lie* is spelled and pronounced the same as the present tense of *lay*:

Present	Past	Past Participle
lie [rest]	lay [rested]	(has) lain [rested]
lay [place]	laid [placed]	(has) laid [placed]

Yesterday Sandra *lay* [*rested*] too long in the sun. She should not have *lain* [*rested*] there so long. Yesterday the workers *laid* [*placed*] the foundation. They have *laid* [*placed*] it well.

like, as. In formal English, do not use *like* (preposition) where *as* (conjunction) sounds right: The old house had remained just *as* (not *like*) I remembered it. It happened just *as* (not *like*) [it did] in the novel. Act *as if* (not *like*) you belong here.

loose, lose. *Loose* (usually adjective—rhymes with *goose*) is the opposite of *tight* or *confined*: The *loose* knot came undone. The lions are *loose*!
Loose is also sometimes a verb: *Loose* my bonds.
Lose (verb—rhymes with *news*) is the opposite of *find* or *win*: Did you *lose* your keys? We may *lose* the battle.

may. See *can*.

maybe, may be. *Maybe* is an adverb meaning "perhaps": *Maybe* Professor Singh will be absent. Do not confuse it with the verb *may be*: He *may be* at a conference.

moral, morale. *Moral* (as an adjective) means "righteous, ethical": To pay his debts was a *moral* obligation.
Moral (as a noun) means "a lesson or truth taught in a story": The *moral* of the story is that greed is wrong.
Morale (noun) means "spirit": Our *morale* sagged.

notable, notorious. See *famous*.

number. See *amount*.

one another. See *each other*.

oral. See *verbal*.

party, person. See *individual*.

passed, past. *Passed* (verb) is from *pass*: *passed* the test.
Past (noun) means "a former time": Forget the *past*.
Past (preposition) means "by, beyond": Walk *past* it.

percent, percentage. Use *percent* with a specific number: 45 *percent*. Otherwise, use *percentage*: a small *percentage* of it.

Note: The *percentage* is singular: The *percentage* of deaths *is* small. A *percentage* is either singular or plural, depending on what follows: A *percentage* of the fruit *is* spoiled. A *percentage* of the men *are* here.

personal, personnel. *Personal* means "private": This is a *personal* matter, not a public one.
Personnel are employees: Notify all *personnel*.

persuade. See *convince*.

practical, practicable. *Practical* means "useful, sensible, not theoretical"; *practicable* means "feasible, capable of being put into practice": *Practical* people with *practical* experience can produce a *practicable* plan.

precede, proceed. To *precede* is to come before: X *precedes* Y.
Proceed means "to go forward": The parade *proceeded*.

presence, presents. *Presence* means "being present; attendance": Their *presence* at the ball was noted.
Presents are gifts, such as birthday *presents*.

principle, principal. A *principle* is a rule or a truth (remember: princip**LE** = ru**LE**): The Ten Commandments are moral *principles*. Some mathematical *principles* are difficult.
Elsewhere, use *principal*, meaning "chief, chief part, chief person": All *principal* roads are closed. At 8 percent, your *principal* will earn $160 interest. The *principal* praised the students.

quiet, quite. *Quiet* means "not noisy": This motor is *quiet*.
Quite means "very, completely": I'm not *quite* ready.

raise, rise. *Raise, raised, raised* ("to lift; make come up") is a transitive verb (takes an object): They *raise* tomatoes. The teacher *raised* the *window*. *Raise* our *salaries*!
Rise, rose, risen ("to ascend") is an intransitive verb (never has an object): The sun is *rising*. Salaries *rose*.

respectfully, respectively. *Respectfully* means "in a manner showing respect": Act *respectfully* in church. *Respectfully* yours.
Respectively means "each in the order given": Use it only as a last resort in clarifying order:
Weak: Brooks, McIntyre, and Singh won the award in 1999, 2000, and 2001, *respectively*.
Better: Brooks won the award in 1999, McIntyre in 2000, and Singh in 2001.

right, rite, write. *Right* means "correct": the *right* answer.
A *rite* is a ceremony, such as an initiation *rite*.
To *write* is to put words on paper: *Write* us from Whitehorse.

sight, site. See *cite*.

since. See *as, because, since*.

sit, set. *Sit, sat, sat* is an intransitive verb (takes no object) meaning "to be seated": They *sat* on the floor.
Set, set, set is generally a transitive verb (needs an object) meaning "to put or place": She *set* her book on the desk. (*Set* is equivalent to *sit* only in regard to a hen's *setting* on her eggs.)

stationary, stationery. *Stationary* means "not moving; not movable": *Stationary* targets are easily hit.
Stationery is writing paper.

take. See *bring*.

teach. See *learn*.

than, then. *Than* (conjunction) is used in comparing: She was more fit *than* he [was]. See 19C(4), page 14.
Then is an adverb meaning "at (or after) that time" or "in that case; therefore": They *then* replicated the study. The vote may be tied; *then* the chair must decide.

that. See *who*.

their, there, they're. *Their* is a possessive pronoun: The litigants arrived with *their* lawyers. *Their* faces were tense.

There is an adverb of place: Sit *there*. It is also an expletive (an introductory word): *There* is no hope.

They're is a contraction of *they are: They're* suing her.

threw, through. *Threw* is the past of *throw*. I *threw* the ball. For *through*, see next entry.

through, thorough, thought. *Through* means "from end to end or side to side of": *through* the tunnel.

Thorough means "complete, exact": a *thorough* search.

Thought refers to thinking: a clever *thought*.

to, too, two. *To* is a preposition: They drove *to* Regina. *To* also introduces an infinitive: They wanted *to* find work.

Too is an adverb meaning "also" or "excessively": They took her *too*. He was *too* old to care. Do not use *too* for *very*: She didn't seem *very* (not *too*) happy.

Two is a number: Take *two* of these pills.

toward, towards. Use either, but be consistent.

uninterested. See *disinterested*.

verbal, oral. Strictly, *verbal* means "expressed in words, either written or spoken": Many computer programs use pictorial instead of *verbal* commands. (For the grammatical term *verbal*, see 14D, pages 8–9)

Oral means "spoken": Give *oral*, not written, responses.

weak, week. *Weak* means "not strong": *weak* from the flu.

A *week* is seven days.

weather, whether. *Weather* refers to rain, sunshine, and so forth.

Whether introduces alternatives: *whether* they win or lose. See also if, whether.

well. See 16C, page 11.

whether. See *if, whether; weather*.

which. See *who*.

while, though, whereas. The basic meaning of *while* is "during the time that." Avoid using it to mean *and, but, though,* or *whereas,* especially if two times are involved: This test proved negative, *whereas* (or *though* or *but,* but not *while*) last month's was positive.

who, which, that. Use *who* to refer to persons; use *which* only for things; use *that* for persons or things: The player *who* (or *that,* but not *which*) scores lowest wins.

who, whom. See 19D, E, pages 14–15.

whose, who's. *Who's* is a contraction of *who is: Who's* that? *Whose* is the possessive of *who: Whose* hat is this?

woman, women. *Woman, like man,* is singular: that *woman*. *Women,* like *men,* is plural: those *women.*

write. See right, rite, write.

your, you're. *Your* is the possessive of *you:* Wear *your* hat. *You're* is a contraction of *you are: You're* late.

SECTIONS 90–96 Paragraphs and Papers

Most sentences that you write will become parts of larger units of writing—paragraphs—and most paragraphs will become parts of still larger units—essays, letters, papers, articles, and so forth. This section explains the basics of writing paragraphs, essays, and research papers, and surveys research paper documentation.

90–91. Paragraphs

Generally, a paragraph contains several sentences clearly related in meaning, developing a single topic. Paragraphs are also visual entities that reduce a page-long mass of print to smaller units more inviting to read.

Paragraphs vary greatly in function, structure, and style. A paragraph of **dialogue**, for example, may contain only a few words (each new speaker gets a new paragraph—see 44H, page 32). A **transitional** paragraph between main parts of a long paper may have only one or two sentences. The guidelines in Sections 90 and 91 apply mainly to **body** paragraphs of expository (explanatory), descriptive, and persuasive papers. **Introductory** and **concluding** paragraphs are shown in Section 93.

90. Paragraph Form and Length. Indent the first line of each paragraph five spaces (2.5 cm or one inch in handwriting), and leave the remainder of the last line blank. The length of a paragraph depends on the topic and its needed development. The typical paragraph runs four to eight sentences, though sometimes one or two important sentences deserve a paragraph of their own. If your paragraph gets too long, break it into shorter paragraphs at a logical dividing point, such as between major reasons or examples.

91. Paragraph Content

A. The Topic Sentence. Develop your paragraph around a single main topic or idea, usually stated in one sentence called the *topic sentence*. Read paragraphs 1–6 below to see how each topic sentence (boxed) controls its paragraph's content. The other sentences generally give evidence to support what the topic sentence asserts. Most often, you will place your topic sentence first—or just after an introductory or transitional sentence. You may also restate or expand upon your opening topic sentence in a closing *clincher* sentence (as in paragraph 4).

You may also place the topic sentence last (as in paragraph 2), with your supporting sentences leading up to it, as to a climax. Sometimes you may need less than a full sentence (as in paragraph 3B) or more than one sentence to state your topic. Occasionally you may just (with caution) imply your topic sentence.

Paragraph 1 (topic sentence first):

Some traditions set aside specific times for telling stories. Among my friends from several Pueblo tribes, stories of Coyote are reserved for winter telling. My *compadres* and relatives in the south of Mexico tell about "the great wind from the east" in the springtime only. In my foster family certain tales cooked in their Eastern European heritage are told only in autumn after harvest. In my blood family, my *El día de los muertos* stories are traditionally begun in early winter and carried on through the dark of winter until the return of spring.

—Clarissa Pinkola Estés

Paragraph 2 (topic sentence last):

To a well-anticipated hanging, if the victims were famous—a Jack Sheppard, a Lord Ferrers—twenty-five thousand people might come. Thirty thousand are said to have attended the execution of the twin brothers Perreau (for forgery) in 1776, and in 1767, eighty thousand people—or about one Londoner in ten—flocked to a hanging in Moorefields.* Against this may be set the extreme unreliability of Georgian statistics. Nevertheless, hanging was clearly the most popular mass spectacle in England; nothing could match the drawing-power of the gallows or its grip as a secular image.

—Robert Hughes

B. Adequate Development. All other sentences in your paragraph should support the general idea you stated in your topic sentence. Many inexperienced writers fail to develop their paragraphs fully enough; they may merely paraphrase the main idea several times or add vague generalizations instead of convincing evidence. Compare the development in paragraphs 3A and 3B below. Which writer better convinces you of what the topic sentence asserts?

Paragraph 3A

The capital of Ghana was very crowded, but that made it all the more interesting. All kinds of vehicles filled the streets. Some of these streets were broad, others narrow and unpaved. Many pedestrians added to the crowded conditions. The mix of children and adults, young women and old men, made this city a colourful one.

Paragraph 3B

Each morning Ghana's seven-and-one-half million people seemed to crowd at once into the

---

*Here the writer refers the reader to an endnote giving the source of his facts.

capital city where the broad avenues as well as the unpaved rutted lanes became gorgeous with moving pageantry: bicycles, battered lorries, hand carts, American and European cars, chauffeur-driven limousines. People on foot struggled for right-of-way, white-collar workers wearing white knee-high socks brushed against market women balancing large baskets on their heads as they proudly swung their wide hips. Children, bright faces shining with palm oil, picked openings in the throng, and pretty young women in western clothes affected not to notice the attention they caused as they laughed together talking in the musical Twi language. Old men sat or stooped beside the road smoking homemade pipes and looking wise as old men have done eternally.

—Maya Angelou

Generally, the body of your paragraph should contain enough specific evidence to support your main idea adequately, convincing even skeptical readers that what you say is true. Your support may consist of **facts** or **examples**; one or more **reasons**; elements of a **description**, **definition**, or **explanation**; events in a **time**, **process**, or **cause-effect** sequence; points of **comparison** or contrast; or more than one of these.

Paragraphs 1 and 2 above are developed with facts or examples. Paragraph 3B uses descriptive facts and some contrast.

Paragraph 4—developed with a reason and contrasts:

Chief among the forces affecting political folly is lust for power, named by Tacitus as "the most flagrant of all the passions." Because it can only be satisfied by power over others, government is its favorite field of exercise. Business offers a kind of power, but only to the very successful at the very top, and without the dominion and titles and red carpets and motorcycle escorts of public office. Other occupations—sports, sciences, the professions and the creative and performing arts—offer various satisfactions but not the opportunity for power. They may appeal to status-seekers and, in the form of celebrity, offer crowd worship and limousines and prizes, but these are trappings of power, not the essence. Government remains the paramount area of folly because it is there that men seek power over others—only to lose it over themselves.

—Barbara W. Tuchman

Paragraph 5 below is also developed with reasons.

C. Coherence. Your paragraphs *cohere* (hold together well) when you clearly signal or imply how your ideas relate to one another—when your thought flows smoothly from the first sentence through the last (and from one paragraph to the next). You can achieve coherence by using (1) a controlling structure, (2) transitions, and (3) repeated key words or phrases.

(1) A controlling structure. Clearly showing your paragraph's structure—its skeleton—helps your reader. This structure can be as simple as labelling your reasons *first, second,* and *third,* as in paragraph 5 below (note the climactic order: the most important reason, labelled *above all,* is last). Paragraph

1 is structured around groups of people (*Among my friends...,* *My compadres...,* *In my foster family...,* *In my blood family...*). Paragraph 2 uses numbers (*twenty-five thousand...,* *Thirty thousand ...,* *eighty thousand...*). Paragraph 6 uses a pyramid.

(2) Transitional expressions:

Indicate stages of thought	first, second (not firstly, secondly), then, next, finally
Introduce particulars	for example, for instance, in particular
Show cause or effect	consequently, as a result, because of these
Signal further evidence	in addition, moreover, furthermore, also
Mark a contrast or change of direction	however, yet, still, on the other hand, nevertheless
Show other relationships	above all, that is, meanwhile, at last, likewise, formerly, more important
Signal a conclusion	therefore, thus, then, on the whole, in sum (avoid the trite *in conclusion*)

You may use all or part of a sentence for transition, either at the beginning of your paragraph or within it:

But the new science could not rely on these pioneers alone. . . .

. . . Despite such difficulties, . . .

Nor is depression the only effect. . . .

. . . In appearance. . . . In actuality . . .

Paragraph 5. Transitions are italicized.*

To be reliable, testimony must be disinterested. *That is*, it must come from a person who does not stand to gain from the statement. If several witnesses swear that they saw the defendant in a robbery case lurking near the bank just before a holdup, the jury is likely to believe them. *On the other hand*, the defence attorney can render their testimony worthless if she can show that these witnesses have something to gain by casting suspicion on the defendant. The question of disinterestedness is not a concern of the courtroom only. It must be considered also by historians trying to establish the truth about the past, legislators trying to draft fair laws, and ordinary citizens trying to determine the credibility of their leaders.

Paragraph 6. Notice how this paragraph begins with a transition linking it to the previous paragraph (*Together these factors . . .*) and is held together by the italicized transitions,* which carry out the writer's idea of a pyramid:

Together these factors produced a unified national band business pyramid that affected black jazz bands. *On the top* were a few very successful

---

*Italics added by the authors of *English Simplified.*

national bands earning excellent salaries and fine reputations. These bands built their names through recordings and radio broadcasts, with careful nurturing by managers. This name recognition was then exploited for financial gain during national tours of ballrooms, nightclubs, and theaters. *On the next level,* less successful national bands followed the same pattern on a smaller scale. *Still lower,* the territory bands continued, but they were definitely marked as minor league, copying the styles of the national bands and losing their most talented musicians to the lure of the big time.

—Thomas J. Hennessey

(3) Repetition of key words or phrases gives your reader valuable signposts to follow the path of your thought. Repetitions may consist of the word itself, a synonym, or a pronoun clearly referring to the word. In paragraph 2 above, note the repetition of *hanging (execution, gallows);* in paragraph 4, *folly, government (public office),* and especially *power.* Repeating a familiar term from the previous sentence near the beginning of your new sentence is especially helpful; in paragraph 6, observe how repetition of *bands* and the use of *These bands* and *This name recognition* helps tie the paragraph together.

D. Unity. *Unity* means that no sentence strays from the topic. Look again at paragraph 4. Imagine the following sentence just after the topic sentence: *Tacitus was a Roman historian who lived from about A.D. 55 to 117 and was known as an eloquent speaker.* Such a sentence would destroy the unity of the paragraph, which is not about Tacitus at all. Look again at paragraph 6. Notice how the image of a pyramid, with its top, middle, and bottom levels, unifies the paragraph.

E. Emphasis. *Emphasis* means that the main points get the most space and stand out clearly, not lost in a clutter of unexplained detail. In paragraph 4, for example, the repetition of *power, government,* and *folly* not only imparts coherence but also keeps the paragraph's emphasis firmly on those three concepts and their interrelation.

92–93. Essays

Just as you build related sentences into paragraphs, you build related paragraphs into longer pieces of writing. One kind—perhaps two to four pages long in college—is an **essay**. Essays allow you to think about and evaluate your own life experiences, observations, thinking, reading, media experiences, and imagination to convey your ideas on just about any kind of topic.

92. Before Starting to Write

A. Choosing and Limiting Your Topic. If you are allowed to choose your own topic or if you are assigned a broad subject, such as campus life, you will have to narrow, or limit, your topic to one that (1) lies within your interests, knowledge, and available resources, (2) will interest your readers, and (3) can be treated adequately within the given length and deadline.

Too broad:	Life on campus
	Cultural diversity in Canadian schools
Limited:	City slicker at a rural campus
	Sharing a room in residence with someone of a different culture
	The parking problem on our campus

One long-range approach to topic-choosing is to keep a **journal** (a daily record) of your experiences and observations. September journal entries can lead to good December essays.

B. Planning Your Essay. Start early and maintain a disciplined schedule, so that you will not have to submit a rush job. Remember: Plans change. At any step, if an idea is not working out or if a better one hits you, revise your topic, your central idea, your plan, or the essay itself. Revising during planning is easier than rewriting later.

(1) Preliminary considerations:

- Your audience. To whom are you writing? Your instructor, of course, but probably also your classmates—or perhaps campus newspaper readers. Consider your audience's probable knowledge of your subject and attitude toward it; fit your content and *voice*—word choice, sentence structure, tone—to your audience.

- Your purpose. Do you want to *explain* the why or how of your topic (exposition)? To *persuade* your audience to think or act differently? To *describe* or *tell* (narrate) something important?

(2) Prewriting. How do you fashion a headful of jumbled thoughts and facts into a coherent essay? Try one or more of these ways (or create your own):

- *Brainstorming.* Just write, non-stop, a *list* of whatever enters your mind on your subject. Do not pause to evaluate or rethink anything, no matter how far-out it seems. Squeeze your brain, as you would a toothpaste tube, to get the last bit out. Then choose your most promising ideas and begin working with them.

- Try *freewriting* if you have difficulty starting. Just start writing, non-stop, *sentences* on anything even loosely related to your subject. Repeat if you have to. Eventually your mind should unlock thoughts on your subject.

- *Mapping (clustering).* Write your subject or tentative topic in the centre of a page. Then, around it, jot down ideas and facts as they come to you; circle each one—bigger circles for broader ideas.

Draw lines between the central subject and the big circles, then between each big circle and the smaller circles that relate to it. Cross out dead-end circles that you find connect nowhere.

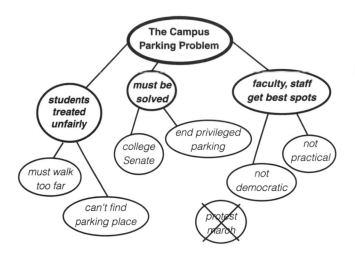

- *Questioning*. Like a newspaper reporter, ask yourself *who, what, when, where, why,* and *how* about your topic.

C. Forming a Thesis. Your essay must not be a mere pile of facts about a topic. Pondering your jotted-down facts and ideas should lead you toward one controlling idea, or point, that you want to convey—what your essay would say if boiled down to one sentence. This is called your thesis. Write a **thesis sentence** stating this point. Be sure the sentence asserts something about your topic (says what you will *show* about your topic).

One path to a thesis is to ask yourself a key question: "What did I learn from sharing a room in residence with someone of another culture?" The answer can become your thesis: "Sharing a room in residence with someone of another culture breaks down preconceptions about other people, brings understanding, and can lead to friendship." (These three effects of sharing can become the three divisions of your essay's body; see 93A(2), page 57.)

Another way to a thesis is to complete this sentence: "In this essay I will show that . . . ." The words following *show that* will form a thesis sentence—how good it is is up to you. (In your actual essay, drop the words *In this essay I will show that.*)

> **Thesis sentence in prewriting:** In this essay I will show that the college must eliminate privileged parking for the faculty and administration because it's not practical, it's not fair, and it's not democratic.

> **Thesis sentence in finished paper:** The college must eliminate privileged parking for the faculty and administration as impractical, unfair, and undemocratic.

Checklist for a Good Thesis Sentence

- Is it a complete sentence? Does it *assert* something about the topic? Is it *one* thesis, not two main ideas?

- Does it fall within the assigned topic range? Does it need to be broadened or narrowed to meet the assignment?
- Will it interest my readers? Does it promise a fresh insight into or understanding of the topic?
- Does it fit my audience and purpose?
- Can it be convincingly supported by my facts and logic?

Compare these thesis sentences:

> ***Poor—no assertion (just a fact):*** This campus is multicultural.

> ***Poor—too broad, stale, dull:*** Harmony among cultures is desirable.

> ***Good—limited, fresh:*** Relations among cultures on our campus differ according to which cultures are interacting.

> ***Poor—broad, unsupportable:*** Everyone on this campus is a racist.

> ***Good—limited, supportable:*** The college administration must take the lead in reducing the widespread but unspoken racism on our campus.

D. Choosing an Approach. Your purpose and thesis will determine how you arrange your ideas. **Narrations** generally follow time order (e.g., A victory over cancer); so do explanations of a **process** (Laying tracks in recording music). **Descriptions** use spatial order (A strip mine); be sure to move consistently left → right, far → near, outside → centre, etc. **Explanations** may follow a simple → complex or familiar → unfamiliar order, or use an *analogy* (a comparison to something familiar: "A blood corpuscle is a tiny balloon filled with a colored protein"—Fritz Kahn). **Persuasive** papers often follow a climactic order: least important reason → most important.

Other approaches: Present a **problem** (campus parking) and give your **solution** (abolish reserved lots); state an **effect** (acid rain) and explain its **cause(s)**, or state a cause (more couples over 35 having children) and consider its effect(s); **compare** or **contrast** two things, preferably point-by-point.

E. Outlining. An outline shows you the sequence and relative importance of your ideas. After determining your approach, make some kind of tentative outline of your essay (stay flexible—change it as needed). At the beginning of any outline, write your thesis sentence.

(1) Scratch outline. Just jot down your main points in the order in which you want them to appear. Leave space between each; in the space below each main point, list supporting items (indented). A variation of this outline is the topic sentence outline: write the topic sentences you intend for each body paragraph. (The scratch outline is good also for in-class timed essays and examination essay questions.)

(2) Branching tree outline:

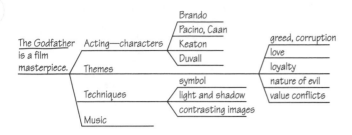

(3) A formal outline uses numbers, letters, and indenting. Your instructor may require one. (You might want to build it from a preliminary scratch or branching-tree outline):

I. Benefits of a large-family upbringing

    A. Development of responsibility

        1. Household

        2. Financial

        3. Societal

    B. Development of social maturity

    (Add C, 1, 2, . . ., D, E . . . as needed.)

II. Drawbacks of a large-family upbringing

    (Add A, B, . . . as needed; III, IV . . . as needed.)

Maintain parallel structure in a formal outline. See 25F, page 21.

93. Writing and Revising the Essay

A. Writing the First Draft. Essays have three parts: introduction, body, and conclusion.

(1) The introduction (usually one paragraph) arouses reader interest, states the topic and usually the thesis, and may suggest the essay's organization. You may arouse interest with a *surprising fact* (Half of Canadian children live in non-traditional families), a *question* (What can account for our endless fascination with the *Titanic?*), an *anecdote* (One day last week I saw . . .), or a *common assumption that you will challenge* (Canadians assume that our health care is the world's best).

(2) The body develops the thesis in several paragraphs (not necessarily the three shown in the sample in section C). What you learned about writing good paragraphs (adequate development, coherence, unity, and emphasis—section 91, pages 53–55) applies equally here. Your thesis sentence may suggest the divisions of your body: . . . similarity of students' (1) *goals*, (2) *ages*, and (3) *interests* encourages cultural understanding. . . .

(3) The conclusion should (re)emphasize your thesis. It may briefly restate your main points and may make a

prediction or suggest action. A good conclusion ends with a strong sentence that both signals "the end" and keeps readers thinking about what you have shown.

In writing your first draft, do not stop to edit for grammar, mechanics, or style. Keep your thoughts flowing.

B. Revising, Editing, and Proofreading. A good essay is usually the product of several drafts and revisions. Improve your drafts by

(1) First, revising—adding, deleting, or repositioning material as needed. Focus on content.

(2) Then, editing—improving coherence, sentence effectiveness, word choice, tone.

(3) Finally, proofreading—checking for errors in grammar, spelling, mechanics, and typing. See 60F, page 36.

C. Sample Student Essay (thesis *italicized;* main divisions in **bold***):

Audience: classmates and other students

Purpose: move them to action

Voice: equal-to-equal, serious, direct, but not pretentious or flippant

Introduction: anecdotal opening to arouse interest and gain rapport; presents thesis and three divisions of topic

Body: a paragraph for each division of topic; each paragraph opens with a topic sentence and transition from previous paragraph (*First of all, In addition, Even if . . . underlying*).

Conclusion: reminds reader of thesis and main points; urges specific action; ends with strong, rememberable sentence.

Unprivileged Parking

    One day last week I had to run a half-kilometre in pouring rain from the student parking lot to my first class. Just outside the classroom building there were over 20 empty parking spaces in the area marked "Reserved for Faculty and Staff Vehicles." Spending the rest of the week in bed with a cold, I concluded that *the college must eliminate privileged parking for the faculty and administration as* **impractical, unfair,** *and* **undemocratic.** Since more than half the students commute to campus by car and all student parking is restricted to the most remote lot,

---

*Italics and boldface added by the authors of *English Simplified.*

beyond the athletic field, the problem is clearly an important one.

Privileged parking for faculty and administration is, first of all, **impractical**. In contrast to the far-off student lot, the close-in faculty-staff lots are often half empty, since the faculty do not come in every day as the students do. Those dozens of empty spaces could be filled with student cars on a first-come-first-served basis, saving dozens of student-hours of time each week. Our time is as valuable to us as a professor's is to her. The student lot is nearly full at peak periods now, and next year students may have to be turned away. Privileged parking is, therefore, an inefficient use of campus space.

In addition, privileged parking is **unfair**, because we students, who must use the outlying lot, have to pay a $25 yearly fee while the faculty, administration, and staff are given the choice spots for nothing. A friend who works in the business office tells me that the fee money is used to maintain the privileged lots as well as the student lots. I have informed my student senator of this gross injustice; she intends to bring it up at the next College Senate meeting. What will the dean of administration say in response to this charge? I and quite a few other students will be there to find out.

Even if the dean can quote some legal loophole by which the college is allowed to use our funds that way, the underlying argument against privileged parking is that it is **undemocratic**. The saying "Rank hath its privileges" is no longer valid today. This is not the Middle Ages, when princes and nobles rode while peasants walked. The faculty may argue that we students are younger and more energetic, whereas some of the more venerable professors may lack the vigour for such long treks. But remember that our student population includes 50-year-old homemakers as well as athletes of 18. Any professor too feeble to make the walk should be given a permit for the handicapped persons' lot (the only justifiably privileged lot) or perhaps should be retired. There is no reason

why a student who has to wake up for an 8 a.m. course must trudge hundreds of yards to class so that a professor who may sleep till nearly noon can fall out of his car into his office.

The fight for **practical**, **fair**, and **democratic** campus parking regulations will be won, however, only if scores of students shake off their apathy and make their voices heard when the motion to end privileged parking is made at next Thursday's Senate meeting. A short walk by these students to Central Hall for this meeting may save countless future long walks to and from the college's own Siberia, the student parking lot.

94–96. Research Papers

94. Planning and Writing. Unlike most essays, research papers are based largely on data gathered from libraries, computer-based sources, and sometimes interviews or other field research. The great amount of work involved demands that you start early, set up a workable schedule, and adhere to it strictly. Rarely are *A* papers written at 4 a.m. on deadline day.

A. Choosing and Limiting a Topic. What was said for essays (section 92A, page 55) applies even more here: *The October Crisis* is a book-length topic, but *How the FLQ kidnapped James Cross* fits research-paper length. You can limit a topic by

- taking part of the whole: choose one of Alice Munro's short stories rather than all
- restricting time, place, or both: not *Canada's foreign policy* but *Canada's NATO policy, 1960–1965*.

A topic must be researchable, not based primarily on personal experience or speculation; it must lend itself to objective, even-handed treatment leading to a conclusion based solidly on your evidence; it must be completable with resources available to you. You will need perhaps ten or more sources, never just one or two.

B. Forming a Thesis. Follow the guidelines for essays, section 92C, page 56.

C. Researching

(1) Traditional print sources include books and periodicals (magazines, newspapers, journals). Locate books through your library's card catalogue, now usually on computer. If you find few or no books on your exact topic (e.g., the technology stock market crash of 2000),

look under broader or related topics (Toronto Stock Exchange, recent Canadian history, finance). You may find a book with some information on your topic; check its index.

Most periodical articles are listed in periodical indexes, such as the *Reader's Guide to Periodical Literature* and subject indexes such as the *Social Sciences Index*. Many indexes are on CD-ROM or on the World Wide Web (through your library's site).

(2) Electronic sources are becoming nearly as important as printed ones, especially for very recent information:
- TV and radio programs, films, video and audio tapes, CDs
- CD-ROMs: compact computer discs of encyclopedias, indexes, and much else
- Online sources: databases; text archives; e-mail; listservs; Usenet newsgroups; IRCs, MOOs, and MUDs; and millions of other sources on the Internet, accessible through **search engines**—such as AltaVista or Northern Light—found on Web browsers.

To look for sources (do a **keyword search**) with a search engine, type your topic in the Search or similar box on the computer screen. Put + or *AND* (depending on the engine) before words you want included, and – or *NOT* before those you want excluded: e.g., *malaria +drug +treatment –quinine; malaria AND drug AND treatment NOT quinine.* Use quotation marks for words you want searched as a group *("stock market crash")*—otherwise you will get data on car crashes and fish markets. To broaden a search you can use *OR,* especially for closely related terms ("stock prices" *OR* "TSE index"); to narrow a search, add more terms *(+Bre-X +TSE +"insider trading")* or exclude some *(–1929).*

> *Caution:* Though the Internet contains many highly reliable sources, such as scholarly journals, it is an ungoverned system: anyone can say anything—perhaps slanted, defamatory, or completely false. Use only sources that seem reliable; avoid personal Web pages, chat rooms, and the like that have no connection to a reputable publisher or institution such as a university or government agency. Be suspicious of data from sources pushing a cause or selling a product (e.g., fitness "facts" from an exercise-machine company). Also, many online sources periodically change their data; write down the date of the latest update and date you accessed the site.

(3) Field work. Some topics lend themselves to gathering original data through interviews, questionnaires, or objective direct observation (such as observing and recording the nursing habits of newborn puppies of different breeds). You may interview an authority in person, by phone, or electronically. In an interview or questionnaire, make your questions concise, specific, to the point, objective, and easily answerable in a form usable in your paper.

D. The Working Bibliography. For each promising source you locate, write on a separate index card the source's *title, author,* and *publishing information* (or the electronic equivalent, e.g., its Web address). See 95, pages 59–65, for examples of needed information. Use either MLA or APA style (or the COS alternative—see 95 introduction, page 59), as your instructor directs. Computer printouts of bibliographies are helpful but cannot easily be merged with your other source items.

E. Taking Notes. Note-taking and planning go hand in hand. With a clear plan you will do less unneeded reading and note-taking; as your knowledge of the topic grows, you can sharpen your plan. In taking notes you may (1) quote directly, (2) paraphrase, or (3) summarize what the source says. Quote sparingly; your paper should be mostly your own words.

Take notes on a separate set of cards from your bibliography cards. Record the page number (if any) of the information, and key each note card to its corresponding bibliography card (e.g., McCulloch, *Trudeau* 287). As best you can, evaluate each source: is it from a known expert and a reputable publication; is it recent, relevant, objective, and convincing? (See also C(2) above).

F. Pulling Everything Together. When finished taking notes, look over your data and revise your outline, thesis, or both, as needed. Arrange your note cards in an order matching your outline, and start writing your first draft. All that has been said about good paragraphs (90–91, pages 53–55) and essays (92–93, pages 55–58) applies here as well.

95. Documenting Your Sources. Research papers, many reports, and articles for publication require **documentation** of all information obtained from books, periodicals, and other outside sources. Documentation consists of (1) **citations**—acknowledgments within your text of sources of materials you used, and (2) a **reference list**—an alphabetical list at the end of your paper of all the sources you used (also called a *works cited* list or a *bibliography*). Generally, papers in the humanities require the Modern Language Association (MLA) style; those in the behavioural sciences and some other subjects use the American Psychological Association (APA) style.* For either MLA or APA style, your instructor may require an alternative form called COS (Columbia Online Style), designed especially to accommodate electronic sources.

---

*APA-based material in sections 95–96 Copyright © 1994 by the American Psychological Association. Adapted with permission.

A. Citations Within the Paper. You must identify the sources of all facts and ideas, including opinions, that you obtain from your research. You must tell enough about each source that your reader can locate the source and the information, and you must always make clear where the source material begins and ends in your text.

(1) The MLA Style. If you cite a *general idea* of an entire work, mention only the author's name in your text (the body of your paper): `Lee traces the chief influences on the history of poverty in Canada since 1990.` [You may add Lee's first name; you *must* add it if you cite two Lees in your paper.]

If you quote, paraphrase, or summarize a *specific fact* or *idea* from a source, cite in your text the author's name and the page from which the material came.

- Direct quotation: According to one recent study, `"Neighbourhoods are often knit together by class and cultural cohesiveness" (Lee 221).` [If your paper cites two authors named Lee, add the first initial.]
- Paraphrase: `Lee observes that a community is often unified by the common culture and social class of its people (221).`
- Paraphrase integrating direct quotation: `Lee observes that "class and cultural cohesiveness" often unites a community (221).`

Your reader can find full information about the source by turning to your reference list:

> `Lee, Kevin K. Urban Poverty in Canada: A Statistical Profile. Ottawa: Canadian Council on Social Development, 2000.` [Canadian Council on Social Development is the publisher]

Note: If your reference list contains more than one entry by the same author(s), give the title (shortened) before the page number in your citation: `(Lee, Poverty 221).`

For electronic sources that have no page, give paragraph number, if any: `(Lee par. 34).` Otherwise give just the author's name: `(Lee).`

(2) The APA Style. If you cite a *general idea* of an entire work, mention the author(s) and year of publication in your text: `Lee (2000) traces the chief influences on the history of poverty in Canada since 1990.`

or

`Another study examined the chief influences on the history of poverty in Canada since 1990 (Lee, 2000).`

If you quote, paraphrase, or summarize a *specific fact* or *idea* from a source, cite in your text the author's last name, the year of publication, and the page from which the material came: `Lee (2000) observes that "class and cultural cohesiveness" often unites a community (p. 221).`

or

`According to one recent study, "Neighbourhoods are often knit together by class and cultural cohesiveness" (Lee, 2000, p. 221).`

Your reader can find full information about the source by turning to your reference list.

Note: If your reference list contains two or more entries by the same author(s) with the same publication year, list these entries alphabetically by title (under the author's name) in your reference list, and in your citations assign each entry a letter in its reference-list order: `(Lee, 2000a).`

(3) The COS Alternative. Generally, follow MLA or APA style but use actual *italics* wherever you would otherwise underline—in your text as well as in citations. For online sources without page numbers, cite just the author's name (in MLA) or name and year (in APA). If no date is given, use the date you accessed the source, in day-month-year form: `(Lee, 4 March 2001).` If the author's real name is not given on e-mail and the like, you may use the login name—the part before @: `(klee@somesite.ca, 16 Apr. 2001);` be sure such a source is reliable.

B. Avoiding Plagiarism. Plagiarism is the theft of another person's words or ideas without acknowledging that person's authorship. Even if unintentional, it is a serious violation of research ethics that can lead to a failing mark. You plagiarize when you either

(1) Use a source's words (even with slight changes) as if the words were your own without citing their source or enclosing them in quotation marks even though you cite the source. Here are two plagiarized versions of the Lee material from A above:

> **Source not identified:** `Two things that hold neighbourhoods together are class and cultural cohesiveness. These forces. . . .`

Source's words not within quotation marks:
```
According to one recent study,
neighbourhoods are often held
together by class and cultural
cohesiveness (Lee 221).
```

(2) Use a source's ideas, even in your own words, without citing that source:
```
A community is often
unified by the common cultural and
social class of its people. These
forces . . . .
```
For legitimate ways to use the Lee material, see A above.

C. The Works Cited/Reference List. Normally, every source you cite in your text must also appear in your reference list, and vice versa. Follow the models in the chart below, noting especially punctuation and capitalization. Section 96, page 66, gives sample pages and details of **alphabetizing** and **indenting.**

Note: The APA's latest guidelines allow actual italics as an alternative to underlining. The MLA, however, prefers underlining. Except in COS, do not use italics without your instructor's permission.

The COS Alternative. If your instructor requires, use the COS variation of MLA or APA form, sampled on page 65. Use actual *italics* rather than underlining. For online sources, give all dates in day-month-year form (1 Apr. 2002) except APA publication dates following author's name (2002, April 1); use no brackets, hyphens, or periods with online addresses. For other sources, follow regular MLA or APA form, but use italics instead of underlining.

Main Differences Between MLA and APA Styles

	MLA	APA
Author	Give names exactly as on title page; if two or three authors, reverse only first author's name (last name first).	Give only last name and initials of all reverse all authors; names. Use & instead of *and*.
Date	Place it with publication data, after title.	Place it just after author name(s), in parentheses.
Title	Use standard capitalization; use quotation marks around short works.	Use no quotation marks; capitalize periodical titles but only first word and proper nouns in other titles.
Indent after 1st line	five spaces	five spaces (or one stroke of tab key); alternative: indent only first line, as in a paragraph (see 96B, page 66).

There are many other minor differences. See samples that follow.

	(1) MLA Style	**(2) APA Style**
Preferred Heading →	Works Cited	References [See 92B for alternative indentation]

BOOKS
One author

Horvath, Polly. <u>Everything on a Waffle</u>. Toronto: Douglas and McIntyre, 2001. [Douglas and McIntyre is the publisher. For university presses use UP: Toronto UP.]

Horvath, P. (2001). <u>Everything on a waffle.</u> Toronto: Douglas and McIntyre.

New edition

Lester, James D. <u>Writing Research Papers: A Complete Guide</u>. 9th ed. Toronto: Pearson, 1999.

Lester, J. D. (1999). <u>Writing research papers: A complete guide</u> (9th ed.). Toronto: Pearson.

More than one author (List authors in same order as on title page.)

Ellis, Gerald P., Lois B. Harris, and Diane Falk. <u>Happy Decisions: The Complete Book of Buying a Dog</u>. Toronto: Holden, 1997. [With two authors, keep the comma before *and*. For more than three authors, mention the first author only (followed by a comma) and then say et al. (meaning and others.")]

Ellis, G. P., Harris, L. B., & Falk. D. (1997). <u>Happy decisions: The complete book of buying a dog.</u> Toronto: Holden. [Use this form for any number of authors. Give names of all authors.]

Editor

Everett, Daniel R., ed. <u>French Canadians: Outside Quebec: A History</u>. Winnipeg: Beaudry, 2000.

Everett, D. R. (Ed.). (2000). <u>French Canadians outside Quebec: A history.</u> Winnipeg: Beaudry.

Author and editor (Ed.) or translator (Trans.)

Layton, Irving: <u>Selected Poems of Irving Layton</u>. Ed. Wynne Francis. Toronto: McClelland and Stewart, 1969.

Layton, I. (1969). <u>Selected poems of Irving Layton</u> (W. Francis, Ed.). Toronto: McClelland and Stewart.

One of several volumes of a book

Edel, Leon. <u>Henry James, the Master: 1901–1916</u>. Philadelphia: Lippincott, 1972. Vol. 5 of <u>Henry James</u>. 5 vols. 1953–1972.

Edel, L. (1972). <u>Henry James: Vol. 5. Henry James, the master: 1901–1916.</u> Philadelphia: Lippincott.

Essay or article in a collection

Lalonde, Maurice. "The St. Boniface Puzzle." <u>French Canadians Outside Quebec: A History</u>. Ed. Daniel R. Everett. Winnipeg: Beaudry, 2000. 37–55. [37–55 = pages in which article is found]

Lalonde, M. (2000). The St. Boniface puzzle. In D. R. Everett, <u>French Canadians outside Quebec: A history</u> (pp. 25–55). Winnipeg: Beaudry.

Bulletin or government publication

Canada. Department of Fisheries and Oceans. Maritimes Region. <u>Science Review of the Dept. of Fisheries and Oceans, Maritimes Region</u>. Dartmouth, N.S.: The Department of Fisheries and Oceans, 2000.

Canada. Department of Fisheries and Oceans. Maritimes Region. (2000). <u>Science review of the Dept. of Fisheries and Oceans, Maritimes Region.</u> Dartmouth, N.S.: The Department of Fisheries and Oceans.

ENCYCLOPEDIA ARTICLE
(If only the author's initials are given see the encyclopedia's key or guide.)

Auclair, Marcelle. "Garcia Lorca, Federico." <u>The New Encyclopaedia Britannica: Micropaedia</u>. 15th ed. 1995. [If no author is given, begin with article title.]

Auclair, M. (1995). Garcia Lorca, Federico. In <u>The new encyclopaedia Britannica: Micropaedia.</u> (Vol. 5, p. 116). Chicago: Encyclopaedia Britannica. [If no author is given, begin with the article title and date.]

PERIODICAL ARTICLES
Magazine article (signed)

Blank, Kim. "Thirteen Ways To Welcome the Millennium." <u>The Sydney Review</u> Dec. 2000: 22–24.

Blank, K. (2000, December). Thirteen ways to welcome the millennium. <u>The Sydney Review 3,</u> 22–24. [3, 22–24 = vol. 3, pages 22–24]

Magazine article (unsigned)

"Junk Diets Not Always Junk." <u>Canadian Observer</u> 22 June 2000: 3.

Junk diets not always junk. (2000, June 22). <u>Canadian Observer, 2,</u> 3.

Journal article (consecutive paging throughout volume)

Kittaneh, Fuad. "Normal Derivations in Norm Ideals." <u>Proceedings of the American Mathematical Society</u> 123 (1995): 1779–85. [123 = vol. 123; 1779–85 = page numbers]

Kittaneh, F. (1995). Normal derivations in norm ideals. <u>Proceedings of the American Mathematical Society, 123,</u> 1779–1785.

	(1) MLA Style	**(2) APA Style**
Journal article (new paging each issue)	Colón, Rafael Hernández. "Doing Right by Puerto Rico." <u>Foreign Affairs</u> 77.4 (1998): 112–14. [77.4 = vol. 77, issue no. 4]	Colón, R. H. (1998). Doing right by Puerto Rico." <u>Foreign Affairs, 77(4),</u> 112–14.
Newspaper article (signed)	Hamilton, Graeme. "Charest Pitches Meech-Like Deal." <u>National Post</u> 14 Jan. 2001: A1+. [A1 = section A, page 1; plus sign means "continued on non-consecutive pages."]	Hamilton, G. (2001, January 17). Charest pitches Meech-like deal. <u>National Post,</u> pp. A1, A3.
Newspaper article or Editorial (unsigned)	"Threat of Lawsuit Clouds Smoking Issue." Editorial. <u>Vancouver Sun</u> 17 Jan. 2001: A12.	Threat of lawsuit clouds smoking issue. [Editorial] (2001, January 17). <u>Vancouver Sun,</u> p. A12.
Review	Walt, Stephen M. "The Hidden Nature of Systems." Rev. of <u>System Effects</u>, by Robert Jervis. <u>Atlantic Monthly</u> Sept. 1998: 130–34. [If the review has no title, just continue with Rev. of . . . after the reviewer's name. If the review is anonymous, begin with the review title, if any; otherwise, begin with Rev. of . . .]	Walt, S. M. (1998, September). The hidden nature of systems. [Review of the book of <u>System Effects</u>]. <u>Atlantic Monthly, 282,</u> 130–34. [If the review has no title, just continue with the bracketed words after the date. If the review is anonymous, begin with the review title, if any, and the date; if no title, use the bracketed words as title.]
UNPUBLISHED WORKS Doctoral dissertation or master's thesis, abstracted	Dunlop, Rishma. "Boundary Bay: A Novel as Educational Research." Diss. The University Of British Columbia, 1999. <u>DAI</u> 61 (2000): 47451. [DAI = *Dissertation Abstracts International*]	Dunlop, R. (1999). Boundary Bay: a novel as educational research. (Doctorial dissertation, The University Of British Columbia, 1999. <u>Dissertation Abstracts International, 61,</u> 47451.
Paper read or speech delivered but not published	Chiang, Yuet Sim. "A Voice of One's Own: Reconsidering the Needs of Non-Native Speakers of English." Curriculum for Cultural Diversity Panel. Conference on College Composition and Communication. Marriott Copley Place Hotel, Boston. 22 Mar. 1991.	Chiang, Y. S. (1991, March). A voice of one's own: Reconsidering the needs of non-native speakers of English. Paper presented at the annual meeting of the Conference on College Composition and Communication, Boston, MA.
ELECTRONIC AND AUDIOVISUAL SOURCES	For the COS alternative, see section 95C, page 61.	
TV or radio program	"How Brains Work." Narr. James Atkinson. Dir. Paul Wrought. <u>Ideas</u>. CBC Radio One, Toronto: 15 Jan. 2000.	Atkinson, J. (2000). How brains work." (P. Wrought, Director). In <u>Ideas</u>. Toronto: CBC Radio One. [Script writer is in author position.]
CD, LP, or audiotape	Morrisette, Alanis. "Front Row." By Alanis Morrisette. Rec. 3 Nov. 1998. <u>Supposed Former Infatuation Junkie</u>. Maverick, 1998. [Begin with the performer, composer, or conductor, depending on your emphasis. If recording is not a CD, add LP. or Audiocassette. or Audiotape. before the recording company's name.]	Morrisette, A. (1998). Front row. [Recorded by A. Morrisette]. On <u>Supposed former infatuation junkie.</u> [CD]. New York: Maverick Records.
Motion picture or videotape	<u>The Sweet Hereafter</u>. Dir. Atom Egoyan. Perf. Ian Holm, Maury Chaykin, and Gabrielle Rose. New Line, 1997. [If a video, after Rose. put 1997. Video-cassette. New Line Platinum Series, 1999. (date of video distribution).]	Egoyan, A., & Cunningham, S. (Producers), & Egoyan, A. (Director). (1997). <u>The Sweet Hereafter</u> [Film]. Hollywood, CA: New Line. [If a video, say Videotape instead of Film.]
CD-ROM or computer disk	<u>The 2001 Canadian Encyclopedia</u>. CD-ROM. Toronto, ON: McClelland & Stewart, 2001. [If a disk, say Diskette and give version, if any.]	<u>The 2001 Canadian encyclopedia.</u> [CD-ROM]. (2001). Toronto, ON: McClelland & Stewart. [If on floppy disk, say Computer Software and do not underline.]
Article or abstract on CD-ROM (If no printed source, give just the electronic source.)	Bloem, Patricia L. "Surviving Stalin to Be Done In by Disney?" <u>Reading Teacher</u> 48 (1994): 272–74. Abstract. <u>InfoTrac EF: Expanded Academic Index</u>. CD-ROM. Information Access, Mar. 1995. [For full article omit Abstract.]	Bloem, P. L. (1994). Surviving Stalin to be done in by Disney? [Abstract]. <u>Reading Teacher, 48,</u> 272–274. Retrieved from InfoTrac EF: Expanded Academic Index. (Information Access, CD-ROM, March 1995 release, Item 16537340). [For full article, omit Abstract. Include item number, if applicable.]

	(1) MLA Style	(2) APA Style
Electronic mail	Culpepper, Daunte. "Why the Giants Beat Us So Badly." E-mail to the author. 15 Jan. 2001.	[Put e-mail communication from individuals as personal communication in the text: D. Culpepper (personal communication, January 15, 2001). Do not include e-mail in the reference list.]
Online posting (listserv, etc.)	Tompa, Peter K. "NUM: 2 Questions about Marcus Aurelius." 28 Jan. 1996. Online posting. NUMISM-L: Ancient and Medieval Numismatics. 8 Apr. 1998 www.umich.edu/~classics/archives/numism/numism.960128.01>. [8 Apr. 1998 is the date you accessed the data.]	Tompa, P. K. (1996, January 28). NUM: 2 questions about Marcus Aurelius. NUMISM-L: Ancient and Medieval Numismatics. Retrieved April 8, 1998 from the World Wide Web: www.umich.edu/~classics/archives/numism/numism.960128.01 [Always include the day of retrieval.]
Personal or professional site or page	"Documenting Sources from the World Wide Web." MLA Style. 7 Sept. 1998. Modern Language Association. 8 Jan. 2000 <www.mla.org/set_stl.htm.> [Add any author or editor as in MLA book style. Quoted part is the page title; underlined part is the site title. First date is that of publication or latest update; second is that of access. If site has no title, give a description, such as Home Page—not underlined.]	Electronic reference formats recommended by the American Psychological Association. (1999, November 19). Washington, D.C. American Psychological Association. Retrieved January 8, 2000 from the World Wide Web: www.apa.org/journals/webref.html [Add any author or editor as in APA book style. If citing a page within the site, begin with the page title (without underlining or internal capitals). Date in parentheses is that of publication or of latest update. If no title, give a description such as Home page—not underlined.]
Article in a professional journal (or its abstract)	Van Dijk, C. Niek, and Nanne Kort. "Telescopy of the Peroneal Tendons." Arthroscopy: The Journal of Arthroscopic and Related Surgery 14 (1998), 471-78. Abstract. 30 Aug. 1998 <www.arthroscopyjournal.org/abs14_5/v14n5p471.html>.	Van Dijk, C. N., & Kort, N. (1998). Telescopy of the peroneal tendons. [Abstract]. Arthroscopy: The Journal of Arthroscopic and Related Surgery, 14, 471-478. Retrieved August 30, 1998 from the World Wide Web: www.arthroscopyjournal.org/abs14_5/v14n5p471.html
Article in a newspaper	Miles, Frank. "Winter Driving and Its Dangers." Arnprior Gazette 9 Nov. 1999 <www.arnpriorgazette.ca/nov9-4/windriv.html>.	Miles, F. (1999, November 9). Winter driving and its dangers. Arnprior Gazette, p. B3. Retrieved December 12, 1999 from the World Wide Web: www.arnpriorgazette.ca/nov9-4/windriv.html
Online book	Duncan, Sara Jeanette. The Pool in the Desert. 1903. Ed. Rosemary Sullivan. Toronto: Penguin, 1984. 14 Feb. 2001. <ftp://sailor.gutenberg.org/pub/gutenberg/etext98/pldst10.txt>.	Duncan, S. J. (1998). The Pool in the Desert, (R. Sullivan, ed.). (Original work published 1903). Retrieved February 14, 2001 from FTP: <ftp://sailor.gutenberg.org/pub/gutenberg/etext98/pldst10.txt

	MLA Style COS Alternative	APA COS Alternative
Electronic mail	Culpepper, Daunte. "Why the Giants Beat Us So Badly." Personal email (21 Jan. 2001).	[Follow regular APA guidelines.]
Online posting (listserv, etc.)	Tompa, Peter K. "NUM: 2 Questions about Marcus Aurelius." 28 Jan. 1996. *NUMISM-L: Ancient and Medieval Numismatics*. www.umich.edu/ ~classics/archives/numism/ numism.960128.01 (8 Apr. 1998).	Tompa, P. K. (1996, January 28) NUM: 2 questions about Marcus Aurelius. *NUMISM-L: Ancient and medieval numismatics*. www.umich.edu/ ~classics/archives/numism/numism. 960128.01 (8 Apr. 1998).
Personal or professional site or page	"Documenting Sources from the World Wide Web." *MLA Style*. Rev. Sept. 1998. www.mla.org/set_stl.htm (8 Jan. 2000). [Add any author or editor as in MLA book style. Quoted part is the page; italicized part is the site. If citing an entire site, use italics only. Last date is that of access. If no title, give a description, such as Home page—not italicized.]	*Electronic reference formats recommended by the American Psychological Association*. (1999, November 19). www.apa.org/journals/webref. html (8 Jan. 2000). [Add any author or editor as in APA book style. Title is that of page (without italics or internal capitals). First date is that of update; second is that of access. If no title, give a description, such as Home page—not italicized.]
Article in a professional journal (or its abstract)	Van Dijk, C. Niek, and Nanne Kort. "Telescopy of the Peroneal Tendons." *Arthroscopy: The Journal of Arthroscopic and Related Surgery* 14 (1998), 471–478. Abstract. www.arthroscopyjournal.org/ abs14_5/vl4n5p471.html (30 Aug. 1998).	Van Dijk, C. N., & Kort, N. (1988). Telescopy of the peroneal tendons [Abstract]. *Arthroscopy: The Journal of Arthroscopic and Related Surgery, 14*, 471–478. www.arthroscopyjournal.org/ abs14_5/vl14n5p471.html (30 Aug. 1998).
Article from an online news source	Miles, Frank. "Winter Driving and its Dangers." *Arnprior Gazette*. www.arnpriorgazette.ca/nov9-4/ windriv.html (9 Nov. 1999). [Give publication date, after Gazette, only if different from access date.]	Miles, F. Winter driving and its dangers. *Arnprior Gazette*. www.arnpriorgazette.ca/nov9-4/ windriv.html (9 November 1999). [Give publication date, after author's name, only if different from access date.]
Online book	Duncan, Sara Jeannette. *The Pool in the Desert*. 1903. Ed. R. Sullivan. Toronto: Penguin, 1984. ftp://sailor.gutenberg. org/pub/gutenberg/etext98/ pdlst10.txt (14 Feb. 2001).	Duncan, S. J. (1903). *The pool in the desert*. R. Sullivan. (Ed.). 1984. ftp://sailor.gutenberg.org/pub/ gutenberg/etext98/pdlst10.txt (14 Feb. 2001).

D. Endnotes and Footnotes. Some instructors using the MLA style may want you to cite your sources by endnotes or footnotes rather than parenthetically as you learned in section 95. **Endnotes** appear in numerical order on a separate page entitled "Notes" at the end of your paper, before the "Works Cited" page. **Footnotes** appear in numerical order at the bottom of the page containing the source material. (Double-space twice between the last line of text and the first footnote.)

In your text, use a raised (superscript) number immediately after the source material. Use the same raised number before the end- or footnote. Number notes consecutively throughout the paper. Single-space within each footnote only; elsewhere, double-space.

In your text (general idea of a book): Lee traces the chief influences on the history of poverty in Canada since 1990.[1]

In the end- or footnote (indent first line five spaces):

[1] Kevin K. Lee, Urban Poverty in Canada: A Statistical Profile (Ottawa: Canadian Council on Social Development, 2000).

Notice several changes from the MLA reference-list form: The author's name is in normal order; book publication information is within parentheses, with no punctuation preceding; commas replace all other periods except the final one.

If you quote, paraphrase, or summarize a specific fact or idea from a source, give at the end of the note the page from which the material came.

In your text: Lee observes that "class and cultural cohesiveness" often unites a community.[2]

In the first foot- or endnote for this source:

[2] Kevin K. Lee, Urban Poverty in Canada: A Statistical Profile (Ottawa: Canadian Council on Social Development, 2000) 221.

In subsequent citations of the same source, use this shortened note form: [6]Lee 187. Or, if your paper cites two or more works by Lee: [6]Lee, Poverty 187.

96. Setting Up the Pages Sample pages of text and bibliography are shown below. Double-space everything. Unless your instructor directs otherwise, make your top, bottom, and side **margins** one inch wide, except for the page number at the top right, which is a half-inch from the top (usually preceded by your last name in MLA style, or the first few words from the title in APA). Many word processors set these margins automatically.

A. Text Pages.

(1) MLA Style. Unless told otherwise, put your heading (your name, instructor's name, class, and date) at the top left of page 1. Centre the title below that; do not repeat the title on subsequent pages:

```
                                    Horvath 1

Emily Rebecca Horvath

Professor Pechter

History 102D

1 March 2001

            Shakespeare's Othello: A World Destroyed

     Near the end of the last scene of Othello, the  play's

title character looks at the man he suddenly realizes

has destroyed him.  Why, Othello asks Iago, why have you done

this? "What you know, you know?" is the sneering answer he

receives.
```

(2) APA Style. Unless told otherwise, start with a separate title page with the following information, centred, above the middle of the page:

Title of paper

Your name, with middle initial

Your school

Count this page as page 1. In the upper right corner of this and every page, put the first few key words of your title and the page number. At the beginning of the first page of text, repeat the title:

```
                              A World Destroyed  2

    Shakespeare's Othello: A World Destroyed

     Near the end of the last scene of Othello, the play's

title character looks at the man he suddenly realizes has

destroyed him. Why, Othello asks Iago, why have you done

this? "What you know, you know" is the sneering answer he

receives.
```

B. Reference List Pages. Alphabetize all entries in one list, according to the last name of the author (if a work has more than one author, alphabetize by the author named first on the title page). If a work gives no author, alphabetize by the first word of the title (other than *a, an, the*).

(1) MLA Style. After the first line of an entry, **indent** all lines five spaces. If two or more entries in a row are by the same author, do not repeat the author's name; type three hyphens and a period (---.). Alphabetize these items by the first word of the title (other than *a, an, the*):

```
                                    Horvath 11

                Works Cited

Blank, G. Kim. The Nature of Evil in Shakespeare's

     Tragedies. Vancouver: Tundra, 1999.

Cullen, Michael. Four Shakespearean Plays. Winnipeg:

     Umberto, 2001.

---. Othello and Iago at War. Waverly, 1999.
```

(2) APA Style. **Indent** in whichever of these two ways your instructor prefers: (1) indent each line after the first line five spaces or (2) indent the first line five spaces and bring the remaining lines to the left margin. If two or more entries in a row are by the same author, list them by date, the earliest first:

```
                         A World Destroyed   11

            References

Blank, G. K. (1999). The Nature of Evil in

    Shakespeare's tragedies. Vancouver: Tundra.

Cullen, M. (2001). Four Shakespearean plays.

    Winnipeg: Umberto.

Cullen, M. (1999). Othello and Iago at war.

    Toronto: Waverly.
```

Alternative APA indentation:

```
    Blank, G. K. (1999). The nature of evil in

Shakespeare's tragedies. Vancouver: Tundra.

    Cullen, M. (2001). Four Shakespearean plays.

Winnipeg: Umberto.
```